Content
DNA.

Content DNA

Cover Design: Col Gray, Pixels Ink
Page Layout: Catherine Williams, Chapter One Book Production

Printed in the United Kingdom

Content
DNA.

John Espirian.

DEDICATION

For Sophie, who has half my DNA
but twice my brains.

You are the moon and the stars
and everything beyond.
You are the grass and the trees
and the earth and the wind.
Believe in yourself.
In what you are. In what you can be.
And in what you will be.

CONTENTS

FOREWORD

I've read plenty of business books and plenty of forewords. Most of them suck because they are airy platitudes for the author or a breathless advocacy for the book.

Why do we need that? The book, and its author, will stand on its own. You are the judge and jury. I honour that!

Instead, I thought I would take advantage of this invitation to set the stage. Why should you read yet another book about content and content marketing?

All of these statements are true:

- Content marketing budgets are skyrocketing.
- Almost nobody can measure it to know if it is doing any good.
- Content marketing is one of the most important innovations in business history.
- Content marketing is grotesquely misunderstood.
- Content marketing is the foundation of my business – I have not spent a dime on paid advertising and neither do most of my customers.
- It is exceedingly rare for most business content to be seen today, and even rarer for it to have a measurable impact on a bottom line. More often than not, it is a waste of money.

So, we need some clear guidance, don't we?

For the last decade, I have devoted much of my professional life to figuring out how we can navigate this marketing minefield and unravel the intoxicating promise of business content. Through hundreds of blog posts, seven years of podcasting, and eight books, I brought many friends along on my long journey.

I needed to discover how to practically make content work for any business, how to find practical success, and the single-most important question in business today: How to stand out in this world of overwhelming Content Shock?

A few people have even listened to me ... and one of them is John Espirian.

John has been a faithful student.

As I pontificated, he has practised.

As I theorised, he has created actionable plans for his own business and beyond.

As I published my books, he absorbed the lessons and created measurable success.

In short, John represents the cutting edge of content marketing reality ... and has developed a few theories of his own.

It is a very proud moment when the student becomes the teacher, and this is one of those moments. It's time to turn over the keys to the next line of thought leaders.

Show us the way, John.

– Mark Schaefer, author of *KNOWN,*
The Content Code and *Marketing Rebellion*

01. INTRODUCTION

A rising tide lifts all boats.
– Fishing proverb

Get to the point

Each chapter starts with the main takeaway. If you're busy or need something to jog your memory, this is where to look.

● ● ●

No one reads the intro anyway so let's get on with it, shall we?

This book's for you if you're a business owner who wants better control over your brand identity and marketing, so that you can be noticed, remembered and preferred in your industry. Even if you hire someone else to implement the tactics to make this happen, you'll understand the underlying lessons involved.

The two big things in Content DNA are the ideas of consistency and congruence: showing up for a long time on a regular basis and being the same "shape" every time when you do.

We'll see how a chance moment led to the creation of a congruent brand for me, and how a considered view of what you want to be known for can mean that you won't need to rely on the same good fortune I did.

You'll define the values that form the building blocks of your brand and come up with content that helps you be noticed, remembered and preferred – to be *the* voice of trust in your industry.

We'll round off with some of the wisdom shared by many of the smart business owners I interviewed when researching this book.

Content DNA is based on the advice I give to my private copywriting clients, to help them create the right footprint in their industry and remain relevant and superior for years to come. My hope is that it can do the same for you.

So, let's get started. What is Content DNA anyway?

02. WHAT IS CONTENT DNA?

DNA is the fingerprint of the 21st century.
– John Walsh

Get to the point

Content DNA is the truth of your business identity. It sets you up for creating content that has its own memorable "shape". It exists to serve businesses that think and act with their long-term interests at heart.

● ● ●

Content DNA is the set of building blocks that defines your business identity. It's what you're all about: the truth distilled and encoded in a few simple messages.

Real DNA is made from just four building blocks, called nucleobases: adenine (A), cytosine (C), guanine (G) and thymine (T). The right combination of these makes you and me and earthworms and bananas. In fact, it makes around ten million different species of living things on this planet. Humans are just one of those species. And yet we show huge variations in what makes us *us*. That's also true for business. No two businesses are exactly alike.

Getting clear on your brand values means finding good

ways to express the truth about you and your business. To show to the world how you're unique. To show that you have a different "shape" from everyone else.

We don't want to be just another grey car sitting in a faceless queue of traffic, moving slowly in the same direction as everyone else. And yet this is the boring, safe way that many of us run our businesses. Well, guess what? No one's going to remember or care about that sort of business. **Boring is the new risky.**

Content DNA is about discovering and embracing the truth about what you stand for and how you're seen. It's about creating and sharing helpful material that has a recognisable shape. It's about being patient and building a long-term presence. And it's about doing it all in an honest, ethical way, avoiding the practices that turn so many people off modern marketing.

Why not just use ads?

Sounds like a lot of effort, doesn't it? Building a brand identity, creating content and playing the long game. I don't blame you for wanting to take shortcuts.

One of those shortcuts is to place ads, the straight exchange of cash money for exposure. Now, this wouldn't be my book if I didn't make it clear that I really can't stand ads. I don't watch them on TV (thanks, Sky+). I don't watch them when streaming (thanks, Netflix). I don't watch them on YouTube (thanks, Skip button).

The well-respected Edelman Trust Barometer[1] says trust in ads is down year on year over the last decade. It also reports that 73% of people surveyed worry about false information or fake news being used as a weapon. Ads that

---

1   https://www.edelman.com/trust-barometer

are often "here today, gone tomorrow" in their nature seem to be particularly good vehicles for mistruth.

Here's the fundamental difference between ads and content, and the reason why I put the latter at the heart of my business. **Ads are a cost but content is an asset.** In fact, content is your time machine: it lets you talk to your prospects far into the future.

Content works for you from the moment you publish it, night and day. Ads work for you, too – but only while you keep paying for them. So, do you want the ongoing cost of ads or the growing asset of content?

When you search on Google, do you pay close attention to the search results marked "Ad" at the top of the page? Or do you scroll past them to get to the useful information you were actually looking for?

Advertising platforms are getting better at allowing you to run targeted ads, which means you can display your ads only to the sorts of people who are likely to be interested in your product or service. That's clearly a good thing, but as this sort of advertising intelligence grows, so does the need to learn how the ad platforms work. Wouldn't it be better to spend that time learning how content could work for you instead?

Ads will help you make a quick impact if you don't have any content to promote yourself. I'd suggest you consider them to help get the ball rolling, but the best long-term strategy is to invest your time, money and energy in producing content that will answer your customers' questions and bring new business to your door.

If you create a good body of content, it will keep working for you forever, even if you take a break. On the other hand, if you use ads and then stop, it'll be like turning off the tap: the traffic to your website will dry up immediately.

The State of Inbound 2015 report by HubSpot found that content-driven marketing "increases leads by 54% when compared with traditional methods, and reduces costs per lead by 13%". Compare this with the growing apathy for traditional ads and you'll see that a content-driven approach to marketing is the sensible way forward.

Good content encourages people to engage with you. And while good ads can get people talking too, they tend to be associated less with helping and interacting and more with broadcasting and selling. Ads drive traffic back to your content. If your content doesn't tell the right story, people won't want to buy from you. The best ad in the world won't be effective for long unless it leads to a strong piece of content. So, whether you use ads or not, you still need good content.

For many businesses just getting started, ads are a good idea. Without an established presence and following, it might take a long time to get any market penetration. Ads can speed up that process. So, I'm not saying *never* to use ads. But I do think that if your business relies mainly or solely on ads, you're going to be at risk from other businesses who do things a smarter way.

Content DNA: the smarter way

Why bother with Content DNA? Because when you have a clear idea of who you are and what you stand for, that makes *everything* easier – for you and your customers. Clear Content DNA reduces friction: it helps more relevant people slide into view – and helps everyone else slide out of the way.

Finding the right Content DNA and then showing it off to the world means you'll attract more of the type of clients you want. They'll like you more than your average customer would. They'll tell more people. They'll complain less. They'll be nicer to deal with. You'll be less stressed when the phone rings.

Do you want all that good stuff for your business? Jolly good. Let's make that happen then. Onwards.

03. MY RELENTLESSLY HELPFUL STORY

Mark Schaefer: How are you fighting to be superior and create that emotional connection in a world with a lot of options?

John Espirian: Relentlessly helpful content.
– Talk at CMA Live 2017 conference

Get to the point

Your brand identity is like the hook of a great song. Get it right and people will echo it back to you.

● ● ●

Being "relentlessly helpful" is at the core of my personal brand. How I stumbled on that label was pure luck. Part of my motivation for writing this book is so that you don't need to rely on similar good fortune.

"Helping your ideas grow."

Back in early 2017, that was my tagline. It was bloody awful.

About a year before then, I'd started studying a topic called content marketing. Through my membership of a UK-based content marketing association, I had a chance to learn about the work of a respected US marketer and author, Mark Schaefer. At that time, Mark was doing research for his book *KNOWN*. His idea revolved around the power of being known in your industry, and it led him to ask a simple question: "Can anyone become known?"

As Mark was looking to interview business owners from all walks of life, he came across me and invited me to chat on a video call. During our conversation, he most bluntly – and helpfully – confirmed that my "helping your ideas grow" tagline was terrible. It was undifferentiated and said nothing about my writing business. The feedback was tough to hear but Mark was right.

The rest of the interview was good and Mark felt there was enough value to him in our chat that he asked to keep in contact and to include me as a case study in his book. I wasn't used to talking with big, important people with decades of marketing experience, so this was a big personal moment for me. To be mentioned in the pages of an actual paper book – imagine! My case study ended up spanning four pages of *KNOWN*.

And it got better: Mark had been invited to speak at a conference in Edinburgh in June 2017, and, as he knew I was attending, he asked whether I and a colleague, personal finance expert Pete Matthew, who was also featured in the book, would be willing to join him onstage. That was another first for me, and I was over the moon to have been asked.

So, there we were, listening to Mark sharing wisdom from his then-new *KNOWN* book and answering some interview-style questions onstage.

Just before we wrapped up, Mark asked me a question that we hadn't planned and that I certainly wasn't ready for.

He asked, "How are you fighting to be superior and

create that emotional connection in a world with a lot of options?" Without thinking, I replied, "By creating relentlessly helpful content."

And that was it. That moment was in large part responsible for why you're now reading this book.

A day or two after I got home to South Wales, a photo popped through my letterbox. Karen Reyburn, a fellow attendee at the conference, had taken a picture of the notes she'd written during the talk with Mark. She'd highlighted "relentlessly helpful content" as her favourite expression, and thought I'd like to see the evidence. I did – and it made me think that maybe there was something interesting in this chance utterance.

I started to use "relentlessly helpful" in some of my marketing materials. Then something unexpected happened: people started to echo the phrase back to me.

In eight years of being in business, not one person had ever echoed my "helping your ideas grow" tagline back to me. I'd never thought about that before, but in hindsight it was a clear sign that those old words weren't wowing anyone.

Since getting a reality check on my initial video call with Mark, I've learned a useful marketing lesson: unless your branding is remembered and echoed, it's not good enough. A tagline and brand message should be like the hook of a great song. Once you hear it, it should stay with you and play back in your head.

Without a good hook for your brand, there's little chance that your clients will listen to the rest of your song. And they certainly won't sing it back to you or others.

Putting "relentlessly helpful" into my marketing was like flicking a switch to turn my microphone on. It meant that people were ready to hear my song, and they've been hearing it regularly ever since.

Now, I was lucky to hit on "relentlessly helpful". Not only did it have something different about it but also it spoke truth to the way I am and how I run my business. When I worked in-house as a software tester and quality assurance manager, I was the guy with the long queue of questioners at my desk. (Perhaps it would have been different had Google been in full swing back then.)

Putting this sense of helpfulness in focus has been transformative for my business. Without that moment onstage and my understanding of its power, I wouldn't be where I am now.

The good news is that you don't need to be onstage in front of hundreds of people to find the right shape for your brand and your business. This book will help you. Once you've found your shape, you'll learn how to create content that catches the attention of the right people.

On we go.

04. WHAT IS CONGRUENCE AND WHY DOES IT MATTER?

By sincerity, a man gains physical, mental and linguistic straightforwardness, and harmonious tendency; that is, congruence of speech and action.
– Mahavira

Get to the point

Create a recognisable shape for your business and stay true to it. Beware of saying, supporting and doing things that give people reason to question your motives. These days, people can sniff a fake from a mile off.

● ● ●

The two key ideas to remember from this book are the need for consistency and congruence. This applies to the way you create content and the way you run your business in general. You probably already have a good idea of what consistency means. We'll get to that a bit later. But what about congruence?

You might have a vague recollection of your maths teacher talking about "congruent triangles". That's when two triangles have the same size, shape and internal angles. If they were made of paper or card, you could stack them perfectly with no sticky-out bits. It's as though they were all drawn from the same stencil or made from the same mould.

So, while the word congruence might not be a word you come across often, you know what it means. It's a defined shape that's always the same. And that's where I want you to direct your efforts – to create a congruent business that is always the same "shape".

Makes sense, right? Except that the shape a business promises to provide quite often isn't the same as the one its customers experience. What's the use of having a load of pretty words and pictures that bear no relation to what a product or service delivers? All this does is set people up for disappointment. If you do that to your prospective and existing customers, you take a big risk. We're ever less likely to tolerate an experience that doesn't match up with what was promised.

So, it's important – I would argue *essential* – that the core product or service you've promised to deliver is in line with the aspirations set by your brand. Now, "brand" might sound like a term that ought to be used only by multi-million-pound businesses, but guess what: your business also has a brand identity, even if you're a one-person operation and your Chief Entertainment Officer is the cat.

Your brand exists in the minds and mouths of everyone who comes into contact with you. What we go through in this book will help you steer people's thinking, by means of a conscious definition of what you stand for and a commitment to be faithful to it in every nook and cranny of your business.

That's what a congruent business is all about. It goes far deeper than giving your website a fancy lick of paint or tinkering with other surface-level changes. DNA is in the title of the book because I want to get to the root of everything that controls how you operate, the same way that real DNA does.

So, here's the harsh reality: a branding exercise on its own won't achieve anything unless it speaks some truth to what's at the core of your business. And even then, it will work only if you apply it as a daily practice. A glossy printout of your brand values is worthless if it's filed away in a drawer and forgotten about.

A congruent brand takes a small handful of truths and demonstrates them all the time and everywhere.

The rise of "cause marketing"

Your principal concern is to create a brand that represents your core business and that serves your customers. You don't need to add to your to-do list by being an eco-warrior or social-justice campaigner. It's the large corporations that tend to walk in this "cause marketing" aisle. It makes sense for them: they have a lot of fans and can influence the way society thinks – and taking a stand can be a real difference-maker.

The scope for your own brand doesn't need to be this broad or world-changing. If there are causes outside your core business that are important enough to you for you to weave them into your brand identity, all well and good.

But don't be suckered into jumping on a "brandwagon" just because you see other businesses doing the same. Draping rainbow colours over your logo doesn't suddenly make you an ally of the LGBT community. I think people are tiring of such virtue signalling.

So, there's your warning: everything in your brand must be part of your DNA. If it's not in your core, show it the door.

Being congruent leads to being known

Content marketing works best when you have a relentless pursuit of being known for one thing. The brand values you come up with through this book, and the content you create as a result of defining those values, will help you achieve that.

Being known is a key step to being *preferred*. And that's where all the success happens. So, let's look next at what you want to be known for.

05. BE KNOWN FOR ONE THING

Be relevant, consistent and superior.
– Mark Schaefer

Get to the point

Focus on one main product or service, one main content creation channel and one main social media channel.

● ● ●

Have you ever been victim of Shiny Red Ball syndrome? It's where something new and apparently interesting comes along and sweeps your attention away from whatever it was you were doing before. It's affected me in the past. It's probably messed with you, too.

Putting a memorable shape into the world means keeping things simple, not trying to do and be too many different things. Your social media presence is a case in point. It's so easy to get excited about the possibility of reaching potential customers that you steam ahead and try to be everywhere.

Before 2017, that's exactly what I was trying to do. Twitter looked cool. *Hmm, let's be on there.* Facebook was popular. *Well, everyone needs a Facebook* presence.

People were getting excited about Instagram. *Oh, I need to try that.* The kids were using Snapchat. *Better understand what's happening there.*

This is the exhausting way to do social media marketing, and it smacks of having no clear strategy. Indeed, that used to be me. I was simply following the herd instead of thinking strategically. Well, I can tell you from experience that trying every new thing definitely isn't the right thing to do.

Having dabbled with every social media platform out there, I realised that I'd never stand out unless I picked a platform and went deep on it. As I work in business-to-business copywriting, it made most sense to try to be known in a space where most potential B2B clients were likely to congregate. That place was LinkedIn.

I was lucky with the timing of my decision. Microsoft had just bought LinkedIn for $26 billion, and changes to the LinkedIn feed helped transform the site from being a place to go only when you needed to change jobs, to being a fully fledged social network.

I found myself in a good place. There was a relatively small user base populated by potential clients, plus excellent reach for the right sort of content. For me, that was written posts. I am, after all, a writer. So, rather than diving into being a podcaster or a YouTuber, I doubled down on writing my blog on my website and sharing the most relevant snippets on LinkedIn.

Despite the favourable conditions for my content on LinkedIn, not a whole lot happened straight away. That's because I was going from a standing start, and it takes time to become known. I'll go into that in the next chapter, when we look at the 30-month mindset.

Jump forward a few years and these days I am indeed

known on LinkedIn. Of the time I spend on social media, 90% of it is devoted to LinkedIn. The other 10% – my bit on the side for dabbling and experimenting – is Twitter.

That 90:10 split of primary and secondary social networks is one of many useful tips I've picked up from my marketing buddies Andrew and Pete. Look out for them on Twitter (@AndrewAndPete) and YouTube – they're fun and smart.

The lesson I've learned from my time in going deep on LinkedIn is that being the same shape everywhere doesn't mean you need to be everywhere. One channel done well is much better than a handful done poorly.

The same is true for content creation in general. Why try to cover all of the bases of writing blog posts, recording audio podcasts, making live and recorded videos for YouTube and creating augmented reality or virtual reality content?

This isn't a sustainable approach unless your business has a proper media arm. And yet I almost fell into the Shiny Red Ball trap again a couple of years ago when I had a chance to take over a technical writing podcast. It sounded like a great opportunity: an existing content channel that had the potential to reach some of my ideal customers. But I didn't have any podcasting experience, and I knew that taking this on would add a lot to my workload.

My marketing mentor, Mark Schaefer, was again to the rescue. I asked him for advice on what to do, and he reminded me to focus on what I was good at. That meant saying no to the podcasting opportunity and staying true to my core value: creating written content. It was a wise decision.

So, I advise you now to pick a content creation channel that you can stick at and that will best serve your ideal audience. It can be easy to flinch when the results of your efforts don't come immediately, but they will if you can be consistent and congruent for long enough. Mark's 2017 book, *KNOWN*, has scores of examples of how this has worked out for people in many different lines of business.

If you do eventually branch out, great. But that should happen only *after* you're already known in one place or for one thing. Have you ever seen someone turn up on a platform and suddenly get loads of followers? There's a good chance that they were already known somewhere else first. They told their existing engaged audience that they were going to be on a new channel and – boom – a large proportion of that audience started following them there. On the other hand, had that person been trying to build audiences on *all* of the channels from day one ... well, that's a heck of a grind.

So, here's what you want to aim for:

- **Be known for one thing**: your core product or service.
- **Use one main publishing format**: blog, podcast, video or other medium.
- **Use one main social media channel**: Twitter, Facebook, LinkedIn or whatever suits you and your audience.

You may have heard the regular refrain of not building your house on borrowed land. I think social media is so pervasive that it's hard to avoid, but don't forget that your social media presence doesn't *belong* to you. If you want to protect your communications with your audience, it's best to create an email list that supplements whatever public messages you put out. That way, should there ever be a meltdown in your social media presence, you can at least fall back on a communications channel over which you have much better control.

Think of your business less like a supermarket and more like a one-dish restaurant. Focus on serving the best dish you can. Stick at it for long enough and you'll become known for it.

How long is long enough? The answer's in the next chapter title.

06. THE 30-MONTH MINDSET

The difference between winning and losing is, most often, not quitting!
– Walt Disney

Get to the point

It takes a lot of time to be known in your industry, perhaps as long as 30 months. Avoid thinking in the short term and get ready to be consistent in the long term. You can win with focus, consistency and grit.

● ● ●

As with anything, diligent practice gives you the best chance of getting results. I'm pretty handy in the kitchen but I'm not a good baker. Still, if I committed to baking a cake every day for a year, you can be damn sure that I'd make something delicious in 12 months' time.

My early efforts would probably be like tough bricks that even the birds would think twice about before they started pecking. Thing is, the delicious version of the cake has the inedible brick as its necessary ancestor. Before you can be good, you have to be bad. It's a phase that all content creators have to go through.

If you can't accept the idea of ever producing an inedible

cake, you might have some mindset work to do around overcoming perfectionism and imposter syndrome. That's not what this book is about, but thankfully lots of clever people have written plenty on such subjects. Try *Ditching Imposter Syndrome* by Clare Josa, for example.

Mark Schaefer's book *KNOWN* showed that it can take 30 months to become known in the right place and space for your industry. I was one of dozens of case studies included in that book, and by following Mark's teachings I've managed to carve out a successful and sustainable business for myself. And, in line with what's set out in *KNOWN*, it did indeed take me around 30 months of hard effort to start seeing the kind of results I was after. I'm telling you this now because I want to put to bed any notion of there being some quick route to success. There is no "easy" button for your marketing.

And yet, a common problem I see with a lot of my copywriting clients is that of impatience: they commission the writing of a few blog posts and then assume that this will magically get them to the top of Google, with plenty of juicy leads to match. Or they commission a whole new website and treat it as though it's a one-off project that gets done and then forgotten about.

The internet doesn't work like that. Any positive effect that comes from a short-term action such as the creation of a new website or small set of blog posts won't last long unless you also have an ongoing strategy for adding new and valuable content for your audience.

Search ranking results come from building a content footprint on your website, fostering a community who will share that material and then getting links back to your site from other places on the web. This takes effort and time – and most businesses aren't ready for it. We'll look later at the kind of content you can create to make sure that your business remains relevant and superior for your ideal audience.

I blogged inconsistently between 2014 and 2016. It got me little in the way of website traffic and almost nothing in the way of leads for my business. It was only when I discovered content marketing in 2016 that I started to buck up my ideas and understand that combining consistency and congruence was the route to success.

Although I focused on writing as my strong suit, it became clear to me that the need for long-term commitment applied to all formats of content. Take podcasts, for example. For the uninitiated, they're digital audio shows, the equivalent of on-demand radio series. Often, people get a bright idea, leap in ... and then quietly bail out. The average number of episodes published across all podcasts is a paltry seven. Yes, just seven! This means that most podcasts barely get off the ground before they crash and burn, and that smacks of little or no strategic thinking.

In contrast, the podcast creators who push through into the triple digits of episodes are the ones who win. My colleagues Pete Matthew and Janet Murray have each had more than a million downloads of the episodes of their respective podcasts. Did they start off with thousands of listeners? Of course not. But they stuck at it. And now, wouldn't you trust that they probably know what they're talking about given that they've published hundreds of episodes between them? Of course you would.

The story is repeated with YouTube video creators, Facebook Live streamers and all other content creators. Consistency is at the heart of all good things worth achieving, whether it's baking a knockout cake or publishing helpful information that serves your audience's needs.

Whatever your aim, you need to make consistency a habit.

About grit

Mark's analysis in *KNOWN* showed that everyone he interviewed had demonstrated a few key characteristics: focus, consistency and grit. I found the last of those words interesting, and it led me to the work of writer Angela Duckworth, who, conveniently, has a book of the same name: *Grit*.

Here's a summary of Angela's recommendations. If you can put these into your business, you'll stand a good chance of being around for the long haul:

- **Find love in your work**: isn't it great to see a small business with excitement and enthusiasm for what they do? We spend much of our waking lives trying to earn a crust. We need to find ways for it to fulfil us.

- **Find capacity to practise**: the best businesses are excellent at execution. You need a way to keep sharpening your blade, not only in the content you create but also in the core service you deliver. Don't just be good: strive to be great.

- **Find your purpose**: think about what's driving you at the root. Money alone probably isn't it. Why are you doing any of this stuff anyway? Clarity on your "why" doesn't matter as much to your customers as some people suggest it does, but it should certainly matter to you. Have a reason to leap out of bed in the morning.

- **Don't lose hope**: business is never plain sailing. Keep afloat. If you've plotted the right course, those choppy waters won't last forever.

We're going to move on soon to define the Content DNA for your business. Before we do, let's see what you can learn from the building blocks I've defined for my business. It's time to check out my Content DNA.

07. MY CONTENT DNA

**The world will ask you who you are, and if you
don't know, the world will tell you.**
– Carl Jung

Get to the point

I use my four Content DNA building blocks in all my content.
This is what defines my shape and helps to make my stuff
memorable (I hope). The building blocks are tied together
with an anchor value.

* * *

My Content DNA is made of four building blocks (plus an
anchor value – we'll get to that in a moment):

- Teacher not preacher
- Cheeky geek
- Attitude of gratitude
- Relentlessly helpful

These are my core four items, and you'll see them
come out in all of my content. They're now so ingrained in
my process that I tend not to need to check that they're
represented when I publish new material.

Ideally, you'll get to the point where you have your own building blocks nailed down and practised so tightly that they'll be naturally present whenever you produce anything for your business. That's when your content will be recognisably *you* – the same shape every time.

For now, here's how my building blocks are made up, how they're expressed and why this matters.

Teacher not preacher

My whole shtick is about explaining how things work. This is what a technical copywriter does for a living: we turn complex subject matter into something actual humans can understand.

Being a good teacher isn't about wagging fingers and making people feel stupid. It's about gently guiding them from "Umm, I don't get it ..." through to "Uh-huh, OK, all right" and eventually on to "Ahh, I wish someone had just told me that before! It makes sense now."

Cheeky geek

Most IT and tech content has clearly been written by girlfriendless nerds. It's deathly boring. I put light-hearted humour in my explainer content to help keep readers awake. This reflects the real me. If I can make you smile, perhaps you'll remember what I'm banging on about.

I use my BitmoJohn cartoon character to add a bit of sass to my content. He's the slimmer, more confident version of me. When things annoy me, he turns into BitmoanJohn and has a little rant. Just wait until chapter 12 where I deliver some smooth slams of social media bad practice.

Humour isn't for everyone but keeping things light and breezy has worked for me. Whatever your Content DNA building blocks are, don't fall into the trap of being dull and grey. Boring is the new risky.

Attitude of gratitude

A lot of people write a gratitude journal, but that feels a bit cheesy to me. I prefer to keep a log of all the positive signals of progress in my business, so I can stay motivated and see where the turning points have been. Doing this is also a good reminder to say thanks – in public and private – to all those who've helped me along the way.

In 2018 I started writing weekly #FridayShout posts on LinkedIn, to put a member of my LinkedIn network in the spotlight, giving them a chance to connect with others and generally raise their profile. As I'm quite a stats nerd, I know that these posts tend to be my poorest-performing ones in terms of views, yet they're a key part of the shape I want to put out into the world – and so they'll stay for as long as I can keep doing them.

I'm also keen to look out for any mentions of my content on social media, so that I can give thanks to the sharers. It's hard to get anyone to talk about your content, so when you find someone who does, it's good to say thank you. Quite apart from it being the nice thing to do, there's no doubt that someone who feels appreciated is more likely to put themselves out for you again in future.

For general comments and shares on social media, YouTube and other places, it's good practice to respond positively. It's so frustrating when content creators treat their platforms and communication channels as though they were for broadcasting only. The key to building an engaged community is to take part in more conversations – and the simple act of thanking someone for contributing a thought or a question can be the start of a new and enriching discussion that helps bring people together just that bit more.

Yes, it takes effort to make sure that no comment is left behind, but it's one of the not-very-secret secret reasons behind my success. Content is the vehicle that drives relevant business conversations. Those conversations and the work that can result from them are the fuel of your business. Ignore them at your peril.

Relentlessly helpful

My original idea for a book was called "relentlessly helpful marketing", but I didn't think that would fill more than a tiny booklet. Honestly, it might even just have been a bullet list:

- Turn up regularly.
- Share helpful stuff instead of selling.
- Be known for one thing.
- Build relationships.
- Don't do stuff you'd hate if it were done to you.

Being "relentlessly helpful" is my take on what is traditionally called content marketing. It's the idea of using content to provide the most helpful, complete answers in a given space, so that you can become the person that potential clients trust the most.

This content helps people make better buying decisions, so while making sales is a natural and positive outcome of sharing such content, the *act of selling* is removed from the process. As someone who hates sales and salesy messages, I'm happy to avoid the unnecessary heart palpitations.

If you *don't* share helpful content that answers people's

questions, someone else will. And the audience that would have come to you will instead end up listening to that other person. That's the way the internet works, I'm afraid.

I know some people are worried about sharing too much helpful content, because they're scared about their competition looking over their shoulders and stealing their ideas and processes.

While it's true that there are some cut-throat businesses out there, I find general worries about direct competitors to be outdated these days. Our real competition comes from the processes and experiences delivered by the best of the best.

In *Marketing to the Entitled Consumer*, author Dave Frankland talks about the "transference of entitlement". It means that companies such as Amazon, Disney and Uber are raising expectations everywhere. Their practices filter through to our way of thinking about what *all* services should be like. When you look at it through that lens, it's short-sighted to worry about what the window-glazing salesperson in the next city is doing.

So, worry less about direct competitors. Focus more on how you can deliver a product or service that addresses a real need, and then share how you do that with the world so that others can benefit from the good you bring.

The anchor value

These building blocks are the core of my Content DNA. I make sure they're at the heart of the way I run my business and that they shine through whenever I create a piece of content.

It's important to express ideas as concisely as possible, and that involves distilling such building blocks into something that sums up the essence of what you're all about.

In my case, the idea of being "relentlessly helpful" is at the root of my identity, and that's the one value I'd want to get across if I had a couple of seconds to speak to someone just as I was exiting a lift and the doors were sliding closed to separate us. (In practice, anyone who waits until the very brink to explain who they are or what they do is probably not too hot at networking.)

What does it all mean?

My Content DNA building blocks and especially my anchor value together represent the shape I'm trying to put into the minds of everyone who consumes my content and who comes into any sort of contact with my business.

These ingredients are what ought to go into the creation of our taglines, which is where we create a memorable descriptor of our business. We'll get on to that in chapter 10.

OK, you've heard about my Content DNA. Now, what does yours look like?

08. YOUR CONTENT DNA

A clear, compelling voice will multiply the impact of your marketing.

– Doug Kessler

Get to the point

Use a variety of methods to find what you stand for. This will define the building blocks for your whole brand identity.

● ● ●

It's important that the building blocks represent you and that they also speak to the positive side of who you want to be and what you want to do. If you can identify the true parts of you that make you excited, you'll have fun building your brand and creating content that expresses it.

If your business isn't the source of some joy in your life, it's probably not going to work. Don't be in that burned-out pile of people who wasted years doing something that just paid the bills. This isn't a call for you to follow your passion: it's a suggestion to think about having fun along the way, whatever you do. Your Content DNA should be something you're proud and enthusiastic to show to others.

As we saw in the last chapter, Content DNA is made

from four or five building blocks that represent your business identity.

So, how are we going to get you to discover what these building blocks are? The best place to start is to take some quiet time to ask yourself what you and your business are all about. This chapter includes some other activities you can do to get to the heart of the real you, so you know how your Content DNA should be constructed.

The mistake that every business makes when it does this stuff for the first time

Almost every business I work with to define their brand values tends to start with a simple list of one-word items. This is quite natural, especially for the analytical B2B company owners who hire me. Few of them have much experience of such work, so it's no surprise to see the way they respond.

The common mistake they make is to fall back on some of the common staples of business: words such as "professional" and "approachable". The problem is that such descriptors are so basic that they don't provide enough of a differentiator. At best, they're "hygiene factors" that should be found in all businesses.

Obvious or undifferentiated terms just aren't going to help you define a recognisable shape for your business. When we're talking about only a handful of Content DNA building blocks at most, each one carries a lot of importance in shaping your presence.

So, forget the hygiene factors. We need to dig a little deeper than that.

Building blocks that are unusual, zany or downright unhinged make for the most interesting Content DNA building blocks. But this isn't a mandate to go nuts: you can play with such exotic building blocks only if they truly represent you. Making things up to sound cool won't work and neither will forcing yourself to change in order to live up to some crazy idea.

You'll need to do some introspection if you're going to unearth what it is that makes you *you*, and then codify that in your Content DNA building blocks so that you can represent a congruent voice in all of your content.

You do need some space to do this properly. Life moves quickly and noisily, and it can be hard to hear the little voice inside that's trying to tell you the truth. Figurative and literal space are useful amplifiers for listening to it.

So, don't be afraid if you need to "get away from it all" for a little bit to get some clarity. (You don't have to grow a beard or buy a dreamcatcher.)

Self-inspection

Think about what matters to you. What do you stand for? What values would you be happy to put your name to? In what ways do your own values show through in how you operate your business?

Consider the ideas that attract you and that repel you. This isn't about changing what you are or even trying to understand why you're built the way you are. I'm suggesting only to observe that which is already true about you, and then to think about how these truths can inform the way you run your business and how to communicate with your audience about it.

What do you believe in? What difference do you make to the lives of the customers you serve? What difference would you *like* to make to them? There are all sorts of these questions you could ask yourself. In an ideal world, I'd tell you to book a few days away in a little country cottage and to spend some time thinking about this stuff. But you're busy and I know you're not going to do that. Grab what quiet time you can and allow these questions to circle in your mind.

This introspection may sound a bit fluffy – and that's the opposite of what I'm about – but it does serve a valuable business purpose. It gives you the chance to look beneath the surface level and glimpse at what real value you're bringing to the world. When we characterise ourselves by our job titles only, we block ourselves from understanding our true value and place.

It's important to know what value you and your business bring to the market, because knowing this is what will help you stay relevant. It's the advice I give to many of my copywriting clients who can be too blinkered or scared to see the bigger picture.

Kodak used to be a giant in the world of photography. But their focus was on selling chemicals on film. If they had instead focused on the bigger picture – *preserving people's cherished memories* – then perhaps they would have become the pioneers of digital photography when they had the chance. They didn't and because of that they've failed to evolve and remain relevant.

That switch in thinking between the practicalities of what you do versus what value you bring comes from knowing your purpose. I don't believe that your customers really care about this, but *you* ought to because it will be responsible for driving your business decisions from now until you think of a different purpose (hint: a single purpose should be sufficient for the lifetime of any business).

Phone a friend

"You can't read the label of the jar you're in." It's a brilliant insight that was popularised by King of Clarity, Steve Woodruff.

It means we can't truly see and understand ourselves without taking into account the way others see and understand us. In fact, it's closely related to Amazon boss Jeff Bezos's famous comment, "Your brand is what others say about you when you're not in the room."

For all that we'd love to have complete control over the way we're seen, we must take into account the impression we've already given others.

Close friends and colleagues can help you by providing an honest assessment of how you show up to them. Don't be afraid to ask their opinions and don't worry if they give you answers that feel quite personal. That feedback could provide insight into your true values.

Identifying your Content DNA shouldn't be a dry, academic exercise. It can take a little pinch of courage to do it right. Notice that all successful content creators tend to be bold and brave in their identity. That doesn't mean being a wild extrovert but rather being willing to be honest and look for the truth.

Also, let's be clear that "brave" is relative here. I'm not asking you to rush into a burning building. I'm asking you to write in a way that doesn't put on a front. If you're waiting for permission to relax and give it a whirl, this is it.

Inspect your content consumption habits

We're all influenced by the content we like. We find it amusing, interesting, truthful, whatever. It speaks to us and we identify with it. At some level, it defines us. And it helps us form bonds with others who like the same thing – it's a positive kind of tribalism.

Think about the shows, films, magazines, websites, podcasts and newspapers that you like. If you were to see a listing of all of those content sources, what would it tell you about the consumer? Forget that it's you we're talking about for a moment. What impression does that list give? Does it portray someone who values humour? Or travel? Or learning? Or social activism?

See what your content diet says about you. In what way could you relate this to your business presence?

Compare these two answer sets for newspapers, films and music:

- *The Guardian*, *Love Actually*, The Bee Gees
- *The Mirror*, *The Purge*, Slipknot

Which would be more likely to choose "agony aunt" as one of their Content DNA building blocks?

Personality tests

If the idea of unstructured self-inspection turns you off, perhaps a more disciplined approach may work better. That's where psychometric tests can help. Here are several for you to experiment with. See what they reveal about you and what might constitute your Content DNA building blocks.

- 16Personalities:
  https://www.16personalities.com/
- CliftonStrengths:
  https://www.gallupstrengthscenter.com/
- HIGH5:
  https://high5test.com/test/
- OCEAN:
  https://www.outofservice.com/bigfive/

- DISC:
  https://www.123test.com/disc-personality-test/
- VisualDNA:
  https://www.visualdna.com/

Your job here isn't to manufacture an online identity. Your job is to recognise and represent your truth – to make a brand that reflects you.

Think about who you're not

What don't you want to be known for? If you think of the values that would repel you if you were a potential customer, the corresponding opposite values might give you ideas about what your true Content DNA is.

This approach can produce a certain sort of sameness in the results (no one would want to be known for being a salesy douche canoe, for example), so be careful not to end up with potential values that are predictably dull.

You might identify "uninterested" as a value you can't stand. You know the businesses who couldn't seem to care less about you. Well, "enthusiastic" isn't the most differentiated opposite to that.

Maybe a better opposite to the yawning customer service person you're thinking of might spark ideas about "always making eye contact" or about "knowing every customer's name".

These are the things that could produce a differentiated Content DNA building block that is referenced in your content and in the way you run your business.

There's more about who your business is *not* for in chapter 22 (Poison portraits).

Your tone of voice

Your tone of voice is your personality put into words. It's natural for this personality to be a central part of your Content DNA.

Content marketing expert and founder of Velocity Partners Doug Kessler says, "A clear, compelling voice will multiply the impact of your marketing. A smart timely, insightful story can be killed stone dead by a flaccid voice. And the same story can go ape-shit viral when told in a bright, surprising, *confident* voice."[2]

One of the most common tone-of-voice questions is, "Is it OK to swear in my content?" The answer is yes, but only if swearing is a reflection of your Content DNA.

It should never be something that you copy from others. Doing that means you can only ever hope to imitate rather than to speak with your own true voice.

So, is it really OK? Sure. If it's you, do it. You'll divide the room and perhaps stop some people turning from prospects into customers, but that's OK. The people who identify with you will probably like you all the more for your honesty.

Doug Kessler is a great example of someone who uses swearing effectively in his content. If you ever hear him do a talk (I've seen him three times now – he's great) then you'll know that swearing is totally congruent with who he is. He's not putting it on and his audience would smell a rat if he were forcing it just to sound cool.

If something is "just not you", don't waste your time by making it part of your Content DNA. For example, "environmental activism" might be a valid building block for some. It's probably not right for you if you own

---

2   https://velocitypartners.com/blog/tone-of-voice-the-b2b-budget-multiplier/

a gas-guzzling 4×4 and do tens of thousands of air miles every year, though.

Remember what I mentioned about cause marketing in chapter 4. Don't support "right-on" things just because it feels cool. Content DNA does not encode well for hypocrisy. This world has enough frauds. Don't be another one.

Now, let's move on and get your brand values nailed down.

09. DEFINE YOUR BRAND VALUES

Your brand is what other people say about you when you're not in the room.

– Jeff Bezos

Get to the point

While your brand is ultimately decided in the minds of those who experience you and what your business brings to the world, you have the control to help direct their thinking. Define the four or five values that will be the building blocks of your brand. These become the shape of your Content DNA.

● ● ●

Your customers and advocates experience your brand. But they are not the sole architects of it. Your brand must reflect the truth about who you are, what you stand for and what shape you want to portray to the world. Doing that right will set you up to attract the people who want to buy from and support you, and then everyone wins.

In the last chapter, we looked at ways to understand what it is you're all about. Now, let's nail that down by picking some real words and phrases to represent your Content DNA.

The aim here is to end up with four or five non-obvious brand values, and then to stay true to them in every single bit of content you create. The brand values should be so foundational to you that you and your business would never act in contravention to them.

The X Factor word list method

Col Gray is a Scottish brand and logo designer. He put together the cover for this book as well as the logo and visual identity you see when you visit my website. Col's method for finding clarity for a brand identity starts with asking clients to review a long list of words and to select around 25 that feel most relevant to them and their business.

From there, the list is reduced by the client in a round-by-round sequence of cuts. Each round of cuts knocks five of the words out of the running. There needs to be some time between the cuts to allow the words to percolate in your mind. Eventually, the final cut should leave you with a final set of five words. It's like X Factor for word lists.

Try it yourself with this short sample list. The full list is on my website. After a few rounds of cuts, you should have a shortlist of words that should be good descriptors of what you're all about.

- Adaptability
- Adventure
- Balance
- Bravery
- Caring
- Creativity
- Directness
- Down-to-earth
- Education
- Expressive
- Fearless
- Fun
- Gratitude
- Hard work

- Humour
- Imagination
- International
- Joy
- Knowledge
- Leadership
- Learning
- Merit
- Motivation
- Neatness
- Open-minded
- Originality
- Passion
- Proactive
- Quality
- Realistic
- Respect
- Satisfaction
- Speed
- Teamwork
- Thankful
- Understanding
- Useful
- Valour
- Vitality
- Warmth
- Wisdom

What's left behind after you finish this process is what Col calls "your compass" or "true north".

For me, it's Content DNA – the building blocks of your identity. This must be the basis of all the content you create.

The celebrity voice method

The methodical option of starting with a long list and narrowing down choices for your brand identity isn't for everyone. When I deal with CEOs and other busy business leaders, they often don't want to make time for anything like Col's exercise. I bang the drum about the importance of making the effort, but I don't pin my hopes on people listening (pragmatism beats idealism at Espirian Towers). So, I give those people a cheat code: I ask them to think about which famous voice they would most want to use in their content.

Imagine you were publishing an important piece of content and you could name one public figure or celebrity whose voice you'd like to use to convey the message. Who would that be? You can strengthen this vision by imagining what it would be like to hear that person narrating an audiobook of the content. Again, who would that be?

For some of the B2B thought leadership stuff I help people with, we often go for an intelligent and engaging voice, such as what we get from John Oliver and Bill Maher on their news entertainment shows in the US.

Maybe you want to channel George Clooney if you're going for a suave, businesslike voice. Or perhaps Martin Lewis for an honest, helpful and rather more British one.

The aim here is to be inspired and to get the content ball rolling. Being a flat-out copycat isn't the point. But as one of the hardest challenges is to start creating stuff, you needn't feel bad about using a crutch like this to guide you through to the early checkpoints in your journey.

Once you're in your flow and have some content creation experience under your belt, it's easier to let your natural voice come out. And when that voice is in tune with the building blocks of your Content DNA, your audience will slowly but surely start identifying with the shape of your content footprint.

In my own case, it took a few years of content creation before I was comfortable enough to let my true voice come out. I'm now at the point where I rarely have to think too much about my own Content DNA, because the building blocks are so ingrained in my process.

All of my content is wrapped in the idea of being relentlessly helpful, with the cheekiness, teaching and gratitude elements playing important supporting roles. That's me in a nutshell and so that has to be my content, too. My content is nothing but an extension of me, so it must carry the same DNA. The same is true for you.

Does everywhere really mean everywhere?

Congruence matters. If you're writing your blogs in one way and then your marketing brochures in another, the best you can hope for is sympathetic customers who assume you have a large team of writers. More likely, they'll wonder either consciously or subconsciously, why you're talking in a different voice.

Apple and Disney don't give their audience such a challenge. Their style is predictable enough that you know exactly what you're going to get, and people appreciate that comfort. It would be weird if either introduced the sort of try-hard comedy lines that other brands use to try to sound cool.

It doesn't matter that the mega corporations have billions of dollars at their disposal. Turning up consistently and being the same shape in your content needn't cost lots of cash. Define your Content DNA and then make it your quality control checklist for every piece of content that your business creates. Given enough time, the "shape" of your content will etch itself into the memory of your target audience.

It's essential to get your Content DNA right in your strategically important content. But it also ought to permeate every part of your business, including how you treat your clients and your staff (if you have any). The 2019 Edelman Trust Barometer[3] reported that 78% of respondents believed that the way a company treats its employees is one of the best indicators of its level of trustworthiness. If you want to earn an audience's trust, being good to your own people is a good way to start. So, please: don't put on a shiny, happy face in public and then

---

3   https://www.edelman.com/trust-barometer

treat your employees like dirt. The cracks will show – and then you'll have a trust fracture on your hands. We'll get to that in chapter 17.

Before that, let's look at one of the most important elements to get right in your Content DNA-powered brand: your tagline.

10. YOUR TAGLINE: THE MEMORABLE HOOK FOR YOUR BUSINESS

An extraordinary claim requires extraordinary proof.
– Marcello Truzzi

Get to the point

Your headline should start with a stock cube of flavour. Put your most important message in the first 40 characters.

● ● ●

Your tagline is the sentence or phrase that accompanies the name of your business. It's meant to be the catchy way to sum up what you do. Problem is, it's tough to come up with something short, representative, memorable and non-cheesy.

That's why copywriters often take as long to write a headline as they do to write a whole article. If an article's headline doesn't grab the right kind of attention, no one's going to care to dig deeper.

The stakes are even higher when it comes to business taglines: get it wrong and you might stop people from finding out more about you at all. Although I didn't fully appreciate it at the time, I was in this exact situation during the period when I had my "helping your ideas grow" tagline.

Your anchor value

Have you identified your four or five Content DNA building blocks? If you've done this properly, you've got short phrases written down for each. It's not a lot of words in total, but it's more than you'd want to trot out if you ever needed to quickly sum up what your business is about.

And no one would naturally say a sequence of phrases without connecting them all together with more words. The whole thing would be a mouthful.

The task is to distil your building blocks down into something that's easier to say. And that's where an anchor value comes in. The anchor value is the foundation on which the Content DNA building blocks sit.

It could either come from emphasising your most important building block, or be something that ties together the rest of your building blocks.

In my case, the building block I'm best known for is also my anchor value: "relentlessly helpful".

Put your anchor value into your tagline

Because your tagline accompanies your business name, it should appear in all of your marketing material, including on your website. That makes it an important and highly visible piece of text.

This is where a lot of businesses fall down, for one of a few reasons:

- **They write something vague**: chuck in a few buzzwords, add "solutions" in there somewhere and hope for the best.

- **They write something cheesy**: it's usually something about how passionate they are about their people and their customers (fine – prove it).

- **They write nothing at all**: there's a missed opportunity for creating a memorable hook for the reader.

Think about what your most important Content DNA building block is and see whether it's strong enough to act as your anchor value. If it is, mould it into a statement of about five or six words, and see how that feels as your tagline.

Remember that it's worth taking a while to get it right. Don't expect to come up with something perfect on your first attempt. Ideally, you want to create at least a few candidate taglines and assess them against each other. If you're part of an accountability group or have close business friends you can lean on, it may be worth auditioning your prospective taglines with them.

Beware of calling yourself an expert: I'm always put off by self-proclaimed experts, and I think Brits in particular are sensitive to this. Focus on doing good things to show your value and let others put the crown on your head. Perhaps even worse than "expert" are the weird titles so often mocked on LinkedIn. Please don't label yourself a "unicorn wrangler", "dream catcher" or anything as fuzzy and unclear as that.

As an aside on tagline length, my tagline is just four words: "relentlessly helpful technical copywriting". I think it's a struggle to get down to fewer words than that, though it's not impossible, and I have some examples of that below.

If you chose a tagline that's just a collection of individual words rather than a phrase, then I'd pick three words, as that seems to be most pleasing to the human ear. For example, business consultant Louisa van Vessem uses "define, grow, transform". This approach is shorthand for a longer statement, so you wouldn't necessarily need to use each word to represent a different Content DNA building block.

If I were to use this approach for my own tagline, I'd probably write something like "heart, humour, helpfulness". But I haven't, because, although I enjoy the alliteration, this doesn't actually tell you what I do. Anything that takes clarity out of a message is definitely a bad thing.

If your most important Content DNA building block doesn't stand well enough alone to fully represent your business, look at the collection of building blocks and see whether there's a common theme to tie them all together. If there is, build a short tagline from there.

If you're still short on inspiration, look at past client testimonials and kind emails and messages from colleagues. What phrases and general themes stand out? See what you can distil and use in your tagline. The result ought to be like a stock cube: something that packs lots of flavour into a small package.

I'm not a fan of making things too formulaic, so I don't want to suggest how you use adjectives and adverbs or anything prescriptive like that. If you think back to the idea that you're coming up with a hook for a great song, you'll know it sounds right when you hear it. I don't think there's a magic formula for that.

If nothing comes to you immediately, don't let this stop you from building a solid presence in the place you want to be known. Sometimes, your actions define your message. Maybe your content will help you see that you're particularly helpful, responsive, unflappable, quick-witted or something else.

An anchor is not a gimmick

Remember that your anchor is your foundation. There's a fine line between being memorable for something authentic and relevant and using a cheap trick. A fancy catchphrase is useless if it has no relevance to what you do. And if no one echoes it back, that's bad.

The shorter your hook is, the better. It carries more weight and is easier to remember and say. Here are some examples:

"Does exactly what it says on the tin." (Ronseal) – eight words
"Because you're worth it." (L'Oréal) – four words
"Every little helps." (Tesco) – three words
"Think different." (Apple) – two words

Remember: your tagline must not be a gimmick or a sales trick. It must be the essence of you, the truth condensed in a stock cube.

Social media headlines

Your social media headline should be in keeping with your main business tagline.

Be aware of what the character limits are and write your headlines accordingly. Just because the space is there, it doesn't mean you need to fill it – but sometimes there's an easy opportunity to improve your findability by adding relevant keywords to your headline.

Aim for a social media headline that is **interesting**, **informative** and **intriguing**.

Let's look at how that works on a 120-character LinkedIn headline, for example.

Headline part 1: "interesting" (40 characters)

The first part of the headline is for your **stock cube**, which packs in the flavour of what your business is about.

Only the first 40 characters of your LinkedIn headline are shown when your posts and comments are viewed on the LinkedIn mobile app. This is the only part of the headline that you can guarantee that people will see (assuming that they read your headline at all).

On LinkedIn desktop, viewers can see about 70 characters of your headline, but with more than 60% of LinkedIn browsing now conducted on mobile, it's better to work with the 40-character limit in mind.

Your tagline – which is based around your Content DNA building blocks and your anchor value – should fit entirely or almost entirely within those first 40 characters.

My stock cube is "relentlessly helpful technical copywriting" (42 characters – hey, I'm not perfect).

Headline part 2: "informative" (60 characters)

The middle part of the headline should be used to expand the Content DNA stock cube, to provide **context** and **keywords**.

In my LinkedIn headline, I've got "for B2B websites. LinkedIn nerd. Author of Content DNA." This provides valuable context so that people know more about what I offer.

Headline part 3: "intriguing" (20 characters)

The last part of your headline is what I call a **bravery badge**. This is your chance to introduce some personality through text that's fun or a little bit out of the ordinary.

Use your bravery badge to amuse or intrigue the reader enough for them to want to find out more about you.

Your bravery badge could be your ideal conversation starter. And the more conversations you have, the more business you're likely to do through LinkedIn. Remember: people buy from people.

My bravery badge is "Not a douche canoe", in reference to the content in chapter 22 about poison portraits.

When I talked about douche canoes in the build-up to publishing this book, it got a strong positive response from my audience. It was fun and I knew people liked it. By including it in my headline, I've given people another opportunity to start a chat with me. If your headline is true and in some way "talkworthy", you're in a good place.

But note that you need to ensure clarity in your word choices. If your headline leaves people scratching their heads, then your attempts at intrigue and individuality may have strayed too far off track. A confused reader quickly becomes an uninterested reader.

Now, let's look at where and how we can enforce our shape.

11. BE THE SAME SHAPE EVERYWHERE

A brand is simply a promise. If that promise is broken, the brand is either not true to itself or not strong enough to keep to the promise.
– Peter Sumpton

Get to the point

Don't assume that a couple of glossy marketing brochures mean you've created a brand. There are lots of ways for your potential customers to experience your brand. Be the same shape every time and in every place.

●　●　●

We've already seen that congruence is the idea of being the same shape everywhere. It's an important part of your business being known, remembered and preferred.

Once you've defined your Content DNA building blocks, your anchor value and your brand tagline, you need to make sure all of it is represented everywhere that people might come into contact with your business. Every touch point should feel familiar and consistent, because your "shape" should always be the same.

Here are some of those touch points and what you

need to think about to make the experience congruent for your audience.

Social media

I recommend focusing almost all your social media effort on one channel, but in practice I know that most people will maintain a presence in more than one place. If that's you and if your social channels have any sort of business angle, it's a good idea to standardise your bio and visuals as much as possible across the board, and to share similar content on each platform. The format of the content might differ, for example you might share text content more on LinkedIn and video content more on Instagram, but the overall feel and messaging ought to be well aligned.

I'd hesitate to say that all bets are off if you're using a social channel for purely personal reasons. If that channel makes you come across as totally different from the business version of you, I'd wonder whether the business version of you is really just a front. Content DNA isn't about that: it's about putting the true you in the shop window. Beware of jarring disconnects between the messages you put out across your social channels.

Email

When people subscribe to your email list, what do you do? The default is usually to send an automated message to confirm that the address has been registered. Wow. What about replacing that with a proper welcome email from you, with links to your good stuff to really get them onboard? What about greeting and thanking subscribers individually via a video-messaging platform such as Bonjoro?[4]

---

4   https://www.bonjoro.com/

I've added a thank you page on my Espresso email signup process so that new subscribers are sent a video welcome by David Brent, star of *The Office* and one of the most famous creations of my comedy hero, Ricky Gervais. The real Ricky wasn't available so I've used an impersonator. Sign up for the list and tell me if he's any good.[5] If you do sign up, one of the lines you'll see in my confirmation email is a polite notice that "Skynet is watching you". It's totally in line with my Content DNA, specifically the "cheeky geek" building block.

Email signatures are a great way to reinforce your brand identity. I use WiseStamp[6] to generate a nice-looking email signature that's consistent when sent from either my desktop or mobile devices. I used to include my logo in my signature. As I'm now building my personal brand, I include the photo that I also use on my website and social media profiles.

Don't forget your out of office messages (if you use them) on your business email. This is a free chance to deliver a memorable message rather than a vanilla response to say that you're unavailable and when you'll be back. It's a touch point so make use of it. Give people something interesting to read or watch until you get back.

Videos

Do you have a standard first frame or thumbnail template, so that all your videos have the same look and feel? If you were viewing them all together on YouTube, would they look like a mish-mash of content? The smart approach is to use a very small number of similar templates so that you can make the

---

5   https://espirian.co.uk/espresso/
6   https://www.wisestamp.com/

videos look quite uniform but still differentiate them subtly. For example, you might have one template for videos that explain a process, another template for answering audience questions and yet another for interviews.

For the video content itself, it's good to use one or a very small number of standard backgrounds. No one's expecting you to run a TV studio, but unless your videos are naturally of the "out and about" style, it's best to keep your environment consistent.

If you use intro or outro segments, standardise them to give your videos a familiar feel. For the videos I share on social media, my standard outro includes audio of my daughter, Sophie, saying, "Relentlessly helpful technical copywriting by my dad." Why? Because it's a bit of fun and it gives people an extra way to remember my tagline. I've had a few nice comments about this approach – it's just another way that I can start a conversation with my audience.

If you add captions to your videos (you really ought to), make sure they're done the same way each time.

Podcasts

If you run your own podcast, keep your production process the same for each episode. That means using consistent cover graphics, show notes, promotional content on social media and intros and outros. It's good to refer to the podcast by the exact name by which it's found in podcast players. It's annoying to hear an imprecise name for a podcast and then not to be able to locate it in a podcast app, then later learning that adding a "The" or "Show" to the search would have returned the right result.

As the host of a show, you have a chance to reinforce

your personal branding in each episode, so describe yourself and what you do in the same terms each time.

If you're a guest on someone else's show, as I often am, send the host a short bio beforehand that contains your photo, tagline and short description. Whatever you want to be known for, make that clear so that the host introduces you correctly to their audience.

Blog posts and articles

We'll talk more about creating good written content later, but the basics of congruence in blog posts are to have a recognisable structure.

I recommend starting the content with a template header image that you customise on each post. This sets a stronger brand tone than opening with a stock image, as so many blog posts do.

If you use in-page menus, buttons and other navigational devices, make sure these are styled the same way in each post.

When you end the post, always use one clear call to action (CTA) that stands out.

All of these things should be defined via the template that governs your website. Keeping the look and structure familiar means that readers can focus on what matters: the substance of your content.

Error messages and microcopy

When things go wrong with your website, don't stick with the generic messages that are displayed by default. Take the opportunity to control what your audience sees.

For example, if someone tries to visit a page on your website that doesn't exist, they will see an error 404 ("page not found") screen. Most websites will let you customise what's shown when this happens. Instead of giving your frustrated audience a standard message, you could write something that relates to your Content DNA, then point people towards the most popular pages and resources on your site. A fun photo and a deliberately overboard grovelling apology can work well, along with a link to your best free content download. Visit any made-up page on espirian.co.uk to see how I handle my error 404 screens.

You may also be able to control the display of other website error messages. For example, the software your website uses to let visitors fill in forms might allow its error messages to be customised. Instead of default error text that tells people that they need to enter their surname or choose an option from a dropdown menu, you might be able to add more human messages.

Even the tiniest bits of text on your website should be in scope for the Content DNA treatment. Think of the short labels that appear on buttons, in menus and in confirmation messages. This is what copywriters refer to as "microcopy" – literally just a letter away from "microscopy", and this is the text equivalent of that.

Such content is often ignored and left with the default text that's part of the website template. This is an opportunity for you to stamp your personality on that text. So long as you don't sacrifice clarity, you can create microcopy that makes the right impression on your audience. Keep talking to them in the voice they recognise as yours.

Voicemail

No one enjoys leaving voicemail when they can't get hold of you on the phone, but you can make the experience better by recording your own greeting and saying something other than "I'm not able to take your call so please leave your name and number and I'll call you back."

A better message might be to remind callers what you do:

- "I'm busy sorting out my clients' accounts before April."
- "I'm working on the world's best marketing plan."
- "I'm building a logo design course."
- "I'm tied up refurbishing vacuum cleaners."

A specific message always beats a general one. I tell callers who miss me that I'm off writing some website copy.

Stationery

If you have branded stationery such as headed paper, compliment slips, envelopes and postcards, think about ways you can reinforce your brand. I use a lot of ticks, stars and thumbs-up symbols in my writing. If you've ever received one of my "good job" postcards, you'll get the drift.

I don't bother with business cards anymore, as I always have my phone with me and much prefer to connect with people I meet in person via LinkedIn. If someone doesn't want to connect with me in the moment on LinkedIn, we probably won't be in contact again. In that case, I don't need to exchange a little bit of card with them that's only going to be fit for the shredder anyway. If you *are* a business card type of person, think of ways you can trade up from handing over a boring rectangular slice of dead tree. I've seen pop-up cards, transparent cards and even cards cut to look like logos. How's that for a literal interpretation of being the same shape everywhere?

In-person networking and conferences

Is your brand represented in some way through the clothing you wear, a mascot you carry or some other visual device that you could use at an in-person event?

I use my BitmoJohn cartoon character in a lot of my LinkedIn content, so when I go to events and conferences, I wear a T-shirt with him on. He's part of my brand and this gets me noticed. I often joke that wearing the shirt is better than any name badge, because it makes me visible from across the room. If you're a regular at in-person events then something like a bold shirt, branded hoodie or other distinctive dress could help you build a recognisable presence.

Some people use plush toys as mascots, giving them selfie opportunities where they might not have had one before. That's not going to work for a lot of brands, but I'm guessing that if you were on the receiving end of it, you'd probably remember having a selfie with the woman holding the squeezy pig (or whatever).

Packaging

If you make a physical product, can the way it's wrapped or presented do more to reinforce your brand identity? It's common to talk about how you're doing your bit to protect the environment (and quite right, too), but are there other opportunities for your tone of voice or values to come across?

Some brands use their packaging to tell little stories that are only loosely connected to the product inside. The drinks company Innocent got attention for printing the words "Stop looking at my bottom" on the underside of their containers. You don't need to be a copycat, but could you create something that makes people want to share a photo of your packaging?

Invoices and receipts

These must be the most boring, personality-free types of content you send to anyone. What better place, then, to liven things up by referring to something relevant to your brand. Are you doing something good to fund social projects? Mention it. Are you big on transparency? Talk about some of the real costs of running your business. I always look to add something light-hearted to my documents. I hope clients will be heartened to know that their delicious cash money is helping my daughter to eat.

Changelogs

If you create software, it's common to publish a running list of new features and fixed bugs. It hardly sounds like stimulating reading but it's becoming more common to see personality seeping into even such normally dry and factual content as this. Put more of this sort of thing into the places where people wouldn't expect to see it. It's the cheapest form of surprise and delight going, but it could mean going from being lumped with everyone else to being noticed, remembered and preferred.

Were those enough examples to whet your appetite for being the same shape everywhere? Apply this idea anywhere that your words or visuals could go, including new media that comes along after you read this book.

Cut through the grey and boring by showing some true personality and being more relatable. These are today's superpowers. None of this has to cost a lot. The admission price is a bit of inventiveness, and the willingness to commit to what your brand really stands for.

Use a consistent photo

It's a good idea to use the same photo in your social media profiles and elsewhere, to help reinforce your online presence. I'm not a fan of seeing totally different shots of someone on LinkedIn and Twitter. If I'm searching for someone on social media, I don't want to have to think, "Is that the same person?" before I go to follow them across multiple platforms. Friction like this does you no favours.

To save yourself a headache, make a list of places to update so that you don't miss anything when you next change your headshot (perhaps once every couple of years). Here are some places to get you thinking:

- Social media
- Google
- Apple ID
- Skype/Zoom

- Dropbox
- Slack
- WordPress
- Gravatar

Your photo is probably in many more places than this. I keep a text file with all my photo locations listed, which is dozens of places, and I store this in the same folder as my headshot so I can update it whenever I need to.

Your photo being in lots of places might increase the chances of someone misusing it. A good way to check whether your photo has cropped up anywhere unauthorised is to use the free TinEye[7] service. I once found that someone from Africa was using my photo in a fake profile, apparently to lure some Japanese women into a scam. Classy stuff.

Speaking of crappy practice, let's move on to take a quick look at some of the bad practice that grinds my gears on social media. If you're doing any of this stuff, don't.

---

7   https://tineye.com/

12. SOCIAL MEDIA BAD PRACTICE

Don't ever try to sell me on anything. Give me ALL the information and I'll make my own decisions.

– Kanye West

Get to the point

Shape your personal brand in a way that doesn't annoy people. Don't engage in social media behaviour that would put you off if you were the consumer.

● ● ●

There's no rulebook for social media. It's a bit like the digital Wild West. People can get away with just about anything. Or at least that's how it can seem at times.

This chapter covers some of my biggest bugbears on social media. Please remember that I'm no sheriff and this isn't the law. That's probably for the best, as I'd surely be a nightmare if I had any real power.

See how much of this you identify with. If we're on the same page, do you ever fall into any of these traps? What can you do to avoid such douche-canoery in future?

Automated direct messages

Don't you hate it when people try to automate authenticity? If you send a private/direct message to someone, don't make it generic. Write a truly personal note or don't bother.

I've seen cases where some automated messages contain deliberate spelling mistakes, so that a subsequent automated message can be used to apologise for and correct the mistake. That's a pretty feeble attempt at making these messages seem real. Who's buying that rubbish? There are already enough real text errors out there without people adding deliberate fake typos.

Conversations are vital in establishing trust with your audience. Don't try to automate them. No one will take you seriously if you do.

Automated replies in public

You know those public acknowledgements on Twitter and other social media: "Thanks for following me, [username]." They suck. Anyone who looks at your feed won't get a good impression. Other automated tweets about "top engaged followers" add no value. If you've set up anything like that, turn it off.

The only good thing about such automated fluff is that you can use Twitter's "muted words" feature to hide such tweets from your feed. I long for the day when LinkedIn offers something similar.

Following, unfollowing, then refollowing

Don't try to game the system to get someone to follow you. Some social media software offers to help you build your social media following. But it does so by making your account follow others. Then it unfollows any accounts that don't follow back within a few days.

This is terrible practice. Decide which accounts to follow based on what interests you. Don't hand this over to an app and let it mess others around like that. Thankfully, the social networks are now curbing the ability of services that do such things.

Not replying to messages

OK, emails often go into spam, but we're talking about social media here. Direct messages tend to be delivered successfully, and you can often see that they've been read. Don't let those messages go unanswered – unless the sender is a spammer or a troll.

Tagging lots of people in posts

On social media, tagging someone in a post means writing their name such that it appears as a link and they receive a notification to let them know that they've been mentioned.

It's OK to ask for opinions in your social content but don't litter your posts with tags. I often mute people who do this, which means I probably won't hear from them again. Don't be that person. No one wants to be a brick in your tag wall.

Tagging is OK if the message is highly relevant to the person being tagged. Often, this happens because the poster wants to get more engagement. That alone is not reason enough to pull someone into your post.

Not tagging the author of content you share

It's good to give credit to an author you cite in your social content. Doing so might even improve the reach of your post. If you post something without crediting the author or source, the reader might assume the content is yours. Curating interesting content is good. Passing it off as your own work isn't. So, show appreciation and tag people when you're sharing something they made or said.

It's annoying when people see what's trending on Twitter or TikTok and then repost it on LinkedIn. Jumping on the viral bandwagon may get you views, but it adds nothing to your credibility.

I've had my content plagiarised before, as have many content creators. It's never a pleasant experience, though it has reminded me that content needs a community to be successful. I remember one example in 2019 when a LinkedIn post of mine was copied and republished without attribution by someone I'd never heard of. While the original post had received 150+ comments from contributors in my community, the copied version received almost no attention (excluding the replies from people telling the chap that he really ought not to be stealing content).

Engagement takes time to build. Warming up your audience and helping them succeed on their own posts is a big part of this, and copycats never bother with that bit, because it's hard work!

You can't copy and paste your way to influence.

Sending generic LinkedIn invitations

That's like putting your business card in someone's pocket and walking away. Come on – send a note. This is easy to do when you invite people to connect via LinkedIn desktop.

On LinkedIn mobile, the Connect button unhelpfully skips the invitation note. To get around that, use the More button to reveal the "Personalize Invitation" option.

(I don't want to get into the weeds of specific LinkedIn features here, because I know it all changes so often. If

LinkedIn have any sense, they'll set things up so that users are prompted to write an invitation note each time they try to connect with someone.)

Requesting endorsements from people you don't know

Don't connect with someone, exchange a couple of messages and assume that's enough to ask them for an endorsement or a recommendation.

If someone connects with you on LinkedIn and immediately endorses you for skills that they couldn't possibly vouch for, that's a strong indicator that they'd like you to do the same for them. If you can't vouch for them, don't reciprocate.

It takes a while to get to know people to the extent that you can be truly confident in recommending them. This is especially true in the online world. Giving recommendations is great and people should do it more often – but only to those they know well.

Adding email addresses to distribution lists

It's happened to us all. We connect with someone, they get access to our email address and then – boom – we're added to their spammy mailing list. Does anyone get business from this? It's an awful practice and I hope the application of the GDPR (General Data Protection Regulation) means it becomes less common.

Respect people's mailboxes and email them via a distribution list only when you have evidence of their explicit consent to hear from you. Also, give people an easy way to opt out of receiving any such emails. If your messages aren't of interest to them, it's best to get them off your list as soon as possible. This reduces your chances of annoying them and gives you more space to engage with the people who are receptive to what you say.

That's enough about bad practice. What about setting out affirmations of how we'll treat our audience? That's where a manifesto is useful.

13. CREATE A MANIFESTO

Live your life as though your every act were to become a universal law.

– Immanuel Kant

Get to the point

Forget me-centric mission statements. Create a document that tells your audience what they'll get from you and your content. Publish it and hold true to those public affirmations.

● ● ●

Some businesses publish a mission statement on their website. It sets out what they're trying to achieve and what's driving them. For me, this whole "start with why" angle has been done to death.

Pages filled with corporate purpose, missions and visions – it all feels a bit too me-centric and self-important. If you have your Content DNA building blocks and a memorable tagline, that's enough. Instead, think about making public promises. This shifts the focus from you to the people you want to serve.

If you had to give your customers three promises right now, what would they be? Assuming you don't already have these promises written down somewhere in public, how would your audience know what they are? They wouldn't have a clue.

I've written a page on my website that I've called a manifesto. It's my flag in the ground to tell my audience what they can and can't expect when they visit my website. Unlike political manifestos, I actually mean this stuff. And unlike politicians, I don't expect to be able to do sneaky U-turns if I get caught breaking my promises.

Here's the deal for visitors to my website. To check the latest version of my manifesto, see https://espirian.co.uk/manifesto.

What my website visitors WILL get:
- Relentlessly helpful content
- Simple, clear language
- Transparent pricing
- Useful referrals
- Captions on videos

What my website visitors WON'T get:
- Spam
- Sales pitches
- Adverts
- Guest posts
- Copying
- Popups
- Image carousels
- Clickbait headlines
- Personal rambling
- Gated content
- Browser notifications

Does any of this sway people? Possibly. Let's look at a couple of these things in more detail.

Popups

There's a growing call for us all to "be more human" in our marketing. A good way to practise that is for us to stop doing the things that annoy people. An obvious starting point for me is website popups. I don't know anyone who likes them. I bet even the people who create them click the "X" button as soon as they see them on other people's sites.

The naysayers will now pop up (ha!) to say that they can't be there to have face-to-face conversations with their website visitors, and so they *have* to show them popups as a way of gathering email addresses.

They'll also say that they *have* to give them a live chat prompt. Oh, and a prompt to allow browser notifications from the website.

I disagree with all of this. Any reasonable person would tell you that these things are annoying. And any data that suggests they work probably doesn't look at the long-term downside for businesses that are associated with taking actions that annoy their customers.

I won't share a post on social media if I know it's loaded with popups and similar annoying features. There's a sharp intake of breath whenever someone sends me a *Forbes* article, because I know I'd need to jump through a few digital hoops before getting to anything interesting.

Gated content

Gated content is online material that you can access only after taking an action defined by the content creator. The usual quid pro quo is, "You give me your email address, I give you a piece of content."

Now, the internet is a big place and a lot of gated content I've seen is – to use the technical term – utterly craptacular.

The aim of such content is to gobble up email addresses as much as possible, but I'm not onboard with this idea. I would rather serve people with the minimum degree of friction, so I put my content out for everyone to access without a barrier.

My website manifesto says: "I won't force you to sign up to my mailing list. If you want my direct help, I charge for my time. Otherwise, all my goodies are free and available to all." Removing the barrier means that more people read my stuff and therefore I have a greater chance that someone will approach me directly or recommend me to someone else. I know this isn't for everyone, though. Each to their own.

(An admission: I have used gated content since publishing Content DNA, to give subscribers to my Espresso list access to a free chapter of this book. I've rationalised that this is fair, given that the book isn't free but almost all my other content is. If you become a Content DNA puritan, you might decide that I've committed a heinous crime here. Sorry.)

Write your own manifesto

Think of the dos and don'ts for your business and your industry. What do you hate and want to see banished forever? Start your manifesto there and cite examples of things you never want to do or be associated with.

Think also of the good things you see. The things you'd want to do more of yourself. Take inspiration from those who are leading your industry. You shouldn't aim to copy, but if someone's doing good and you're not, think about the reasons. Why should you keep doing things your way?

If you can't think of a reason, maybe you need to do that good thing, too – or at least whatever your version of it is.

Then, look beyond your industry. What are the good and bad practices you see in other places? What can you learn and apply? Remember that people aren't comparing you with other businesses in your industry. They're comparing you (perhaps subconsciously) with the best experiences they have in every other field.

Once you have a basic manifesto, publish it. Allow others to hold you to account for it. Show that you mean what you say by staying true to your affirmations, and prove that your word is your bond.

Now, let's get into some tips for creating good content. Pull up a CHAIR and let's do it.

14. PULL UP A CHAIR

If you are silent about your pain, they'll kill you and say you enjoyed it.
– Zora Neale Hurston

Get to the point

Until you work out your Content DNA building blocks, the CHAIR framework is a useful safety net for creating content that engages your audience.

● ● ●

Your content should always have the same "shape", else you risk it being too fuzzy to be remembered by your ideal audience.

But what if you're not yet crystal clear on your Content DNA building blocks? Well, then you could do with a ready-made safety net. Or rather, a CHAIR.

Here's an acronym to keep in mind:

- **C**hallenging
- **H**elpful
- **A**musing
- **I**nteresting
- **R**elevant

Until you nail down your final set of Content DNA building blocks, this CHAIR will prop you up. Check that you're hitting at least a couple of the following before you publish any piece of content.

Challenging

By this I really mean you should challenge people's thinking. Posing subjects from different and interesting angles can lead to your audience coming up with their own insights on things they might not otherwise have stopped to consider.

Without getting too *Inception*-ish about this, it's good to seed ideas in your audience's mind such that it feels to them as though they arrived independently at a conclusion you were already hinting at.

Challenging content can also be more divisive, and this sort of material often performs well in the echo chamber of social media. This approach works only if you're OK with people deciding that they really can't stand your guts.

Please don't go picking fights with your content. Use your keyboard to connect and collaborate, not to cajole and crush.

Helpful

Put the needs of the reader before your own. Instead of publishing self-serving "me, me, me" content, think about how best you can serve your audience. What would help them most right now?

One of the best reactions I get to my content is along the lines of "I can't believe I didn't know that. Thank you so much!"

When you're an expert in your field, you know things that your audience doesn't. Share that knowledge and watch those lightbulbs fire in people's heads.

Amusing

Stuffy and boring isn't going to cut it anymore. Copywriting 101 is to make your content conversational. Most of us have some humour in what we say, so don't be afraid to let that come out. If you write the way you talk, you're likely to make a better connection with your audience.

Before 2016, I used to play quite a straight bat with my content. In hindsight, it's no surprise that it didn't resonate as well as my stuff does now. It was still me, but me in a straitjacket. I've since learned to break free of those restraints. You can do the same.

Half of 1000 marketers surveyed by Sprout Social in 2019 said social media posts that entertain were more effective in helping them reach their goals than discounts and sales content.[8] Think about that: giving people money off is not as effective as making people smile.

This doesn't mean you should race to the other end of the spectrum. Don't try to be a comedian if you're not. People will see through the cracks. Instead, become comfortable with letting your personality show. Think of your content as a big conversation with your friends.

Interesting

Your content doesn't have to offer Hollywood levels of entertainment (thank goodness or else I'd be screwed), but it should pique your readers' interest enough to make it worth remembering and, ideally, sharing.

Good content is talkworthy and shareable. As Mark Schaefer says, "The economic value of content that isn't seen or shared is zero." Make your stuff interesting enough that your audience will make *themselves* look good by sharing it.

---

8   Sprout Social Index 2019: https://sproutsocial.com/index/

Relevant

Relevance is essential if you want to become known as the voice of authority and trust in your field.

I can think of a couple of people who get a lot of views on LinkedIn by sharing viral content they've scraped off Twitter. Do I know their names? Yes. Do I know anything about their businesses? Not really. Would I buy from them or recommend them to others? Definitely not. Don't be someone else's "definitely not". Stay mostly on topic (*mostly* because all work and no play makes Jack a dull boy) and be remembered for the right reasons.

On social media, be careful what you like and comment on. Even if the content you create is relevant, you still risk exposing people to irrelevant content you've interacted with. If you take my approach of going deep on a single social platform (LinkedIn, in my case), make sure that platform represents what you want others to see and learn about you.

Get off your CHAIR

Once you have your Content DNA building blocks nailed, put those at the front and centre of your content creation.

That doesn't mean doing away with the good things in CHAIR – it would be stupid to stop producing relevant material, for example – but rather focusing more on the values that are going to reinforce your own unique shape.

CHAIR is general enough to apply to anyone. Your Content DNA should be specific enough to apply only to you.

Now, let's move on to an uncomfortable truth for all you people-pleasers: not everyone will like you.

15. NOT EVERYONE WILL LIKE YOU

If people are not going to like you it needs to be because of who you are not because of who you are trying to be.
– Vicki O'Neill

Get to the point

Our marketing should be magnetic: it should attract but also repel. If we have interesting opinions and if we stand for something, not everyone will buy into that – and that's perfectly fine.

● ● ●

If you're a people-pleaser like me, this chapter title is a nightmare. I was raised to serve others and to seek approval from them. That meant doing what I could to help people and to get them to like me through doing that. Not offending people and not complaining were big parts of that. I'd be annoyed or upset if people didn't like me.

Here's the problem: if you try to please everyone, you won't make a strong impression on anyone. Being a chameleon or a doormat isn't the path to being remembered or respected.

It's much better to plant your flag and say, "This is me and this is what my business is about." This approach is useful for a couple of reasons. First, it sends a clear signal to a large proportion of the viewing public and says you're not for them. Second, it sends an even clearer signal to a much smaller proportion of the viewing public and says that you definitely *are* for them.

Think of a room containing 100 people. You could be a vanilla people-pleaser in an attempt to do business with most of the room. Perhaps you'd be of mild interest to half of those people. But if you can have a more distinctive shape to your presence, you might be of strong interest to five or ten people. The rest of the room won't be interested at all. Sounds nuts? Think about that small number of people being your fans. They're the people who'll sing your praises and do your marketing for you. That attracts other people like them and can even attract people from the large original group who weren't interested.

In *Marketing Rebellion*, Mark Schaefer's research reveals that two-thirds of our marketing isn't done by us – it's done by our customers. This loss of control over our marketing is what the book is about, and it's something we should embrace in our Content DNA. Be your own distinctive shape and attract the customers who are nuts about your style. They'll pay you more, be more loyal and spread the word about you. That small proportion of the room is powerful. Speak to them and stop worrying about the rest.

I know this sounds tough. What if you're leaving money on the table? But by focusing on that small group of fans, you'll have a better business that keeps attracting better customers. If you're in a stack 'em high, sell 'em low business, perhaps you don't care. But if your product or service offers something of value and has a price that reflects this, you want your efforts to be received and appreciated by the *right* people.

By positioning your message to exclude a lot of the room, you leave space to spend more time with the people who really go nuts for your stuff. Bonus: doing business with your raving fans means that you're much more likely to get their understanding when things go wrong, and they're far less likely to complain in general. Oh, and did someone say lower support costs?

Embrace your enemies

We can't please everyone. Memorable brands tend to have a divisiveness about them. This doesn't mean you have to actively seek hatred and trolls, but you do need to make clear who you're for and who you're not for.

I use a fun, friendly and cartoony way to promote my technical copywriting business. For potential clients who want technical content that's safe and played with a straight bat, I'm probably not the right guy. My visuals and my tone of voice should be enough to get this across to them very quickly. I'm fine with that because I'm not interested in working on dull, run-of-the-mill jobs. My branding provides those potential clients with the "road closed – take alternative route" sign they need so that they don't waste their time and mine on having an ultimately fruitless conversation.

Unless you take steps to make your identity clear, you risk being the beige option that tries to appeal to everyone. This is terrible for being memorable and will lead to work that doesn't inspire you. So, as counterintuitive as it might feel, it's good if some people are put off by your position in the market. It's even better if they really can't stand your guts, because that means it's more likely that there will be people at the other end of the spectrum who lap up everything you do. Keep in mind that your position has to be based on staying true to a defined set of values and also must be focused on bringing some value into the world. If that weren't the case, you could just come up with some abhorrent views and be done with it.

Beware of alienating your people

It's OK to divide the room. You should do that.

But you have to make sure you're on the side of the people you want to work with. Alienating people who would genuinely be your potential or actual customers is stupid.

The attempt to move Weight Watchers to become WW: Wellness That Works felt disingenuous and was confusing, so much so that they had to reintroduce the term Weight Watchers. Imagine if they'd been more honest: "We don't want to focus on weight because it's not woke enough. And besides, Oprah wants us to change."

If you know your customers well enough, you can be confident that taking a stand and expressing your own truly held beliefs and opinions will work out. Look at Nike. They're known for speaking out. When they came out in support of Colin Kaepernick, an American footballer who'd been protesting the treatment of racial minorities in the US, a lot of people thought they'd lost the plot. Their share price tumbled, and the gloaters pointed out what a PR fail the whole incident had been. But Nike knew what they stood for and that their position would resonate with their audience. Little more than a week later, their share price was above where it had started.

Nike had divided opinion. Those against them increased their dislike for the brand. But those who were already on their team felt even more of a shared identity with them. They saw their beliefs reflected in the position of a brand they already liked. What did it mean? Even more respect, loyalty and sales for Nike. They could have stayed quiet and avoided the controversy. But they didn't because they knew themselves and they knew their customers. Taking a stand was actually a safe bet – and it worked.

The same principle applies for businesses much smaller than Nike. If you know what you stand for, you'll attract the sort of people who think the same way. Not everyone will like what you do and that's absolutely fine.

Every time I send an email to my Espresso list, I can guarantee that a few people will unsubscribe. It's just the way of things. If I were fearful of offending people, it would be safer not to send anything to them at all. No unsubscribers that way!

But that's entirely the wrong way to look at it. A personal brand must stand for something. If you have an approach that's remotely interesting, there will be people who like you and those who don't. We don't need to appeal to everyone and we shouldn't even try.

What's for sure is that staying silent isn't going to influence anyone. Speak up and divide the room. Some people just won't like you. Make peace with that fact as soon as you can.

Remember also that our marketing should be magnetic: it should attract but also repel.

I've told you in this chapter not to be a chameleon and to embrace knowing that some people won't like you. That can be most apparent when we're face to face. So, let's look at that most dreaded of things: meeting people in person.

16. MEETING PEOPLE IN PERSON

Always be a first rate version of yourself and not a second rate version of someone else.
– Judy Garland

Get to the point

Make your online persona match your offline one, and vice versa. Being a social chameleon may have given your ancestors an evolutionary advantage. That doesn't need to restrict who you are now. Be unapologetically you.

● ● ●

Isn't it great when you meet someone in person and they're exactly the same as they are behind a computer screen? You can relax and enjoy their company because you know what to expect.

But then there are the let-downs – the times when a person you thought was pretty cool online actually turns out to be a grade-A douche canoe.

You start questioning yourself. Was your judgement wrong? Did you say something to upset them? Maybe they just don't like you? It's no fun to be in this state of uncertainty, and uncertainty is the enemy of trust.

Now, ask yourself: would you ever want to raise those questions in the mind of someone else?

Living by your Content DNA means being the same shape everywhere. It means that the way you are online is the same as you are in person. It means that if someone likes the online you, they'll like the offline you. Because it's all *you*.

I've been on the internet for more than half my life. No matter how appealing someone's online persona is, I try to reserve my final judgement about them for when we meet in person. Video chats get you close to the truth of a person, but there's nothing quite like being in the same room. The challenge for us all is to make our online presence be faithful to the experience of being eyeball to eyeball with us. Hand on heart, is that true for you?

Sometimes, the differences between a person's online personality and their in-person behaviour can be down to them having an introverted nature. The safety of a screen and a keyboard gives them the freedom to be the real them online, but they feel less bold in face-to-face social gatherings.

So, keep in mind that the differences you perceive between someone's online persona and their in-person vibe could be explained by their natural introversion. But don't just give people an automatic "get out of jail free" card. Sometimes, it's clear that you're not dealing with the same person, and not because of shyness, hesitance or any of the other things that might hamper personal interactions.

It can also go the other way. Sometimes you'll meet someone in person who doesn't particularly stand out online. It can be nice to discover someone like that, but I always wonder how much better off they'd be if they could show that same personality online.

Beware of being a social chameleon. This may have been a good evolutionary trait to have had – the ability to fit in quickly with a different social group would be a way to stay safe and avoid isolation. But that same ability might hinder you from developing a memorable personal brand. Your real DNA has brought you here, but it doesn't need to be the sole arbiter of how you act from now on.

As marketing legend Seth Godin would say, no one will take notice of just another cow in the herd. But a purple cow stands out. (*Purple Cow* is one of his bestselling books.) Be faithful to your own shape and don't be quick to smooth out the corners too much. If you're to be authentic in any meaningful way, keep those chameleon urges at bay.

As a recovering people-pleaser, I've struggled with this for a long time. If you don't want others to feel discomfort or awkwardness, it's easy to adapt the way you talk and behave to suit them. Doing so ingratiates you with them. And it can drain the hell out of you.

But remember: not everyone will like you, and that's OK. Be unapologetically you, online and offline.

17. TRUST FRACTURES

**It takes twenty years to build a reputation and
five minutes to ruin it.**
– Warren Buffett

Get to the point

Make everything you do an act of reinforcing the trust
between you and your audience. If they trust you and you
don't mess things up, you'll be unstoppable.

● ● ●

We're in a world where the availability of information is at an
all-time high, and where switching costs are at an all-time
low. In the 2020s, if a business messes you around, you can
get up and flounce out of the door.

If you want to avoid such hair-tossing happening to
you, you need to do everything you can to build and keep
trust with your clients and your audience. When that trust
fractures, it happens more publicly than ever before. We're
at peak peril for customer loyalty.

Twitter and other social media have accelerated the
possibilities for reputations to be destroyed. People are
better than ever at sniffing out fakes and businesses who

don't live up to their stated goals and missions. If you're a douche canoe, you're not getting away with it anymore.

Serve up a bad experience to the wrong person and they might make you Instafamous for the wrong reason. This is one of the reasons why PR firms that specialise in crisis management are still in operation.

Lead with imperfections

It's natural to put your best foot forward, to focus on the good stuff so that you can impress your audience. We all do it.

But here's an interesting challenge to that intuitive wisdom. If you start your communication with an admission of where you're not absolutely smashing it, you have the chance to build more trust with your audience.

In *The Transparency Sale*, author Todd Caponi reports research that shows that buyers are most likely to buy products that have imperfect ratings. Using the common 5-star rating system, products with a 4.2–4.5 rating are more likely to be bought than those products with a perfect 5.0 score.

Think about it. Have you ever seen something look so perfect that you start to wonder whether it's really all it's cracked up to be? And then think of the iPhone: a product that has sold millions of units and that's beloved by countless people around the world. But this slice of Jobsian wonder doesn't get perfect ratings, because it's not perfect – and nothing else is either. Even *Harry Potter* gets 1-star ratings sometimes.

The insight from *The Transparency Sale* is clear: leading with flaws and authenticity can increase trust and shorten buying cycles.

If you're like me, you'll wince a bit when thinking about how to apply this to your own product or service. And yet here we are, wincing together at the thought of mentioning anything like that in public. Rather than admitting that you suck at one task or other, a more positive way to frame the information is to talk about what you can't do for clients.

For example, if you work from home and live away from the big cities, your lifestyle might mean you don't want to be travelling to some smog capital to meet people face to face. And in that case, maybe you make a point of saying that you handle consultations online only because you no longer book in-person meetings.

Is that a limitation that will put some clients off? Yes. Will your other clients appreciate your honesty? Yes. You can't do everything for everyone. Being clear about boundaries and limitations is fine. Transparency isn't a mandate for self-flagellation. Don't be afraid to share relevant truth. People will respect you for it.

There's another challenge to be aware of. The mean-spirited reader might look at the above and come up with a troubling idea: why not fake it? Why not manufacture a flaw in your business and use that as some kind of hook? Remember the way no one suspected Keyser Söze in *The Usual Suspects*, because of the physical characteristics that he was putting on? He was the nice guy – until he wasn't.

Of course, we're all imperfect, but if we misdirect attention to the things that will somehow make us look good rather than being honest about where we're truly not up to standard, that's A Bad Thing. I'm not sure what the answer is, but I know that sniffing a fake could lead to a massive public trust fracture.

Mark Schaefer's most recent book, *Marketing Rebellion*, talks about the second customer rebellion being "the end of lies". It means we can't sweep things under the carpet anymore. So, please: don't put yourself in trouble by lying about or hiding flaws in your products or services. Leading with honesty is the smarter way into people's hearts and wallets.

A quick aside: *The Transparency Sale* is one of dozens of great marketing books I first learned about via the Marketing Book Podcast, run by Douglas Burdett. If you don't have much time to read, you can get great summaries of books and listen to interviews with their authors by subscribing to Doug's weekly show. I find it an amazingly effective way to stay up to speed with what's happening in the world of marketing. And it's free.

Show evidence of people's trust in you

"You have to eat there. We went last night. That buffet … just … it's ridiculous. We've got the loyalty card and everything. Are you coming next week?"

"YES! Getting the extra-loose trousers ready for that one. Call me."

We all know that the best recommendations come from face-to-face chats with people we trust. We can't expect this to happen with everything ("You won't believe how powerful these industrial lift motors are. Get over here, Bill!"), so we have to rely on reviews and recommendations.

Whether you have a product or a service, there are a few places I recommend focusing on to help your potential clients see that you're worth dealing with.

LinkedIn recommendations

Unlike testimonials that you add to your website, LinkedIn recommendations have to be submitted by the person recommending you. They can do that either by visiting your profile and using the Recommend option, or they can respond to a request you send them to recommend you.

I find that the most heartfelt and honest recommendations are those given freely and without any prompt or expectation from the receiver. The only downside is that the recommendation text can be a bit woolly and not specific enough to influence the intended reader.

The most effective recommendations tend to be those that show evidence of some tangible benefit or change brought about by the recipient's product or service. For example, "it was great to work with Louisa" would be far better if upgraded to "Louisa set up a couple of diary-management processes that saved us ten hours last week." One of these is fluffy and nice; the other might actually get the phone to ring.

When your LinkedIn connections show willingness to give you recommendations, you might be able to help them and yourself by suggesting words, phrases or even complete sentences for them to use. So long as they're happy to put their name against such statements, I see no problem in helping them with these suggestions.

The recommendations your connections submit appear on your LinkedIn profile as soon as you've authorised them. You also have the option to request tweaks before authorisation, but that's not the same as editing the text yourself.

Website testimonials

Once a LinkedIn recommendation is on your profile, I suggest asking for permission to republish it somewhere on your website. If the recommendation-giver agrees, copy some or all of the text and place it on your site, along with the name, headshot photo and website link of the giver.

I used to do this without a photo or by including a corporate logo instead of a personal image. But faces are trusted more than logos or blank spaces, and these testimonials look a lot more human and trustworthy when they're associated with a real person.

The big mistake a lot of website owners make with testimonials is lumping them all together on a single page. If you've ever done this, look at your website analytics and I bet you'll find that that testimonials page barely gets any traffic. People just aren't interested in trawling through this sort of content.

It's far better to spread your testimonials around your website, putting the best ones on pages that receive a lot of traffic. Think also about placement of the testimonials on the page. If you have a big button on the page that is asking the reader to buy a product or subscribe to a course, wouldn't it be great to have a relevant and positive testimonial appear near the button? Small decisions like this can have a big impact on how well your website converts visitors into customers.

Google reviews

We all want our businesses to be found easily when our prospective customers search online for our products and services. A good way of improving our chances of being found is to encourage people to leave reviews on Google.

To allow this, your business needs to be registered for the free Google My Business service. This involves jumping through some verification hoops, possibly including the latest "innovation" I've heard of from Google: asking you to take part in a quick video call to show photographic evidence of your property and car registration details(!)

This sounds like a hassle – and it is – but it's worth the effort for the benefit of allowing your customers an independent space to provide star ratings and written reviews for your business.

Just as we pay attention to restaurants and hotels with good ratings and reviews, so we do with businesses. And with Google My Business, you'll be listed on Google Maps just like everyone else. This can apply even if you don't have a physical store and all your work is done remotely, as mine is.

One more thing: your Google My Business settings will let you generate a short web address that you can send to colleagues and customers to encourage them to rate and review your business. I've done this and you can see the result here: https://g.page/espirian/review.

These are far from the only places to gather positive feedback from your customers. Depending on what your business offers, your reviews might appear on Amazon, eBay, TrustPilot, Checkatrade and many other sites. Consider how customers interact with your business to ensure your reviews are being added and seen in the right places.

Above all, remember that even thousands of positive reviews won't protect you from potential trust fractures. But if you always put your customers' needs first, you'll never need to worry.

18. PATTERN INTERRUPTS

Whoever can surprise well must conquer.
– John Paul Jones

Get to the point

Consistency is good. We don't have enough of it in our businesses. But leave space for surprise and delight. A splash of pink goes well with all that white paint.

●   ●   ●

Although I think consistency is a good thing and that our businesses all need more of it, there's probably some danger in being remorselessly uniform and entirely predictable. If you really operated in a completely cookie-cutter fashion, your people would all sound identical and devoid of any individuality. It's the equivalent of turning your business into a vending machine, and that doesn't feel right.

If Mark Schaefer's marketing mantra of "be more human" is to mean anything, we have to understand that Content DNA isn't about sucking the personality out of your people and replacing it with four or five brand values that they must hammer home to the exclusion of everything else. Instead, we should see Content DNA as a deep and important thread that weaves through everything you do – but it's not something intended to turn people into mindless clones. There's still space for humanity and personality. In fact, that's what's missing from so many non-memorable businesses.

If we really want to leave a lasting impression on our customers, we must do whatever we can to improve their experience of our products and services. That can mean doing the things that don't always scale well. This can help build emotional connections that make you immune to changes in pricing and other fluctuations in the market.

Create a peak moment

Can you create a peak moment for your customers? Something in the process of dealing with you that's special enough to be remembered and talked about? In *Talk Triggers*, marketing author Jay Baer gives examples of unexpected and unusual acts that are turned into business-as-usual activity by innovative companies.

One example was of a Californian restaurant, Skip's Kitchen, where the customers get the chance to pick from a deck of cards when they place their order. If they get the joker, their meal is free. Whether they get lucky or not, the promotion is inventive enough to warrant them mentioning it to friends and family afterwards. Combine that "talkworthiness" with a good core service and you get a business that's bound to attract more customers. Think about what your "joker in the pack" routine could be.

Even if you can't bake something into your business-as-usual process, there's nothing to stop you adding some surprise and delight for your best customers and closest advocates. There's no good dashboard for measuring the power of being nice and going out of your way for someone. And there's no guarantee that kind acts will reap their rewards – but then this isn't meant to be a business transaction. Try doing good things anyway and see what comes of it.

Somewhat out of the blue, my marketing buddy and fellow Liverpool FC fan Peter Sumpton sent me a Champions League final programme in June 2019. We'd connected on LinkedIn well before we realised that we both supported the same team. Even though we'd had prior contact, Peter took it to another level through a kind and – most importantly – meaningful act. He could have sent me £20 in the post and that would have been nice, but it wouldn't have been memorable, and it certainly wouldn't have got him a namecheck in this book.

Peter has become a strong advocate of mine. He champions my message and has invited me on his podcast, The Marketing Study Lab. He'd probably lend me the shirt off his back if I asked (not that it would fit). Who wouldn't want someone like that in their network?

Here's another example. When I realised that two of my favourite LinkedIn connections, marketing and sales expert Vicki O'Neill and LinkedIn guru Jeff Young, lived in the same US state of Ohio, I introduced them online. They got talking and soon got to meeting in person. They kindly recorded a public thank you video and posted it as a surprise. Even more kindly, they sent me a "douche canoe" mug from across the Atlantic, in honour of one of my favourite phrases. Now, that's what I call going above and beyond – creating a peak moment for me to cherish and smile about every time I take a sip of coffee.

Here's the lesson: learn something non-businessy about your clients. It might be something about sport, art, family, social causes or anything else. Find ways to bring that into your relationship with them. Perhaps nothing may come of such gestures, but if you make an effort with a genuine desire to help people, there's a genuine chance that it will pay off.

The network building I've done since I threw myself into LinkedIn at the start of 2017 means that I now have loads of great advocates. They're the committed contributors who get my content seen and who leap to the front of the queue when I put my book up for pre-order. These are the people who you want to find and develop relationships with.

But getting back to peak moments, why do they matter, especially for people who are already buying from you? Why not invest that energy in finding even more customers to do business with? It's all very well having fans of your content, but fans don't pay the bills. Getting new customers through the door does. Right?

Well, it's much easier and more powerful to nurture relationships with existing clients (and advocates) than it is to hunt for new buyers. Here are some stats[9] shared with me by copywriter and LinkedIn business coach Heidi Medina:

- It costs five times as much to acquire a new customer as it does to keep an existing one.

- Increasing customer retention rates by 5% increases profits by 25% to 95%.

- The probability of selling to an existing customer is 60–70%, but the probability of selling to a new prospect is 5–20%.

- Existing customers are 50% more likely to try new products and spend 31% more, when compared with new customers.

---

9   https://www.invespcro.com/blog/customer-acquisition-retention/

You need to make sure your current clients feel loved, always. Once you have your core group, you'll have enough to sustain your business. If you ever alienate those people, that's a sign that you're drifting away from your Content DNA.

Remember that your advocates are the accelerators to getting new business. Take care of them just as much as you would an existing paying customer. In fact, the better you treat them, the more likely you are to attract the interest of others who want to be part of your tribe.

Recover strongly and finish well

If you drew a graph of someone's customer experience with a business, it wouldn't always be a straight line. There would be bits they liked and bits they didn't like. The graph would be at least partly squiggly.

Bizarrely, inconsistent experiences like that might improve customers' overall impression of a business, so long as the final outcome is positive. In other words, a mess-up followed by redemption is OK, but awesomeness followed by a kick in the teeth isn't.

A bit of adversity in the customer experience provides an opportunity to recover and impress people. There's even an argument that says that customers who have been treated well after having had a bad experience can end up being great advocates for the business. But please don't take the cynical view and try to engineer something like this into your process.

Even if you're able to maintain your standards and not drop the ball anywhere during the process, aim to end your transactions on a high point. This would also be the time to take advantage of your privileged moment to ask for a recommendation or referral.

Making the most of the moments where your

customers are most likely to be happy is precisely why Disneyland ratings and feedback are so good immediately after the grand fireworks display at the end of the day. The same people giving those glowing ratings wouldn't have done the same if they were asked to share their thoughts near the start of the day, when all they could see were countless tired parents shepherding impatient toddlers around a never-ending human maze.

So, in summary, look for opportunities to go above and beyond as a way of strengthening bonds with customers and advocates. End on a high and ask for feedback at the right time.

19. CONSUME, CONTRIBUTE, CREATE

There could be shadow galaxies, shadow stars and even shadow people.
– Stephen Hawking

Get to the point

First you watch. Then you chip in. Then you *do*. This is the pathway from lurking to leading. Be brave and take the steps to become a creator, because creators get all the glory.

● ● ●

In most online user communities, those who create content get the most visibility. Think of anyone you admire in the public sphere. Chances are, they'll have created something you like. They might be an actor, a musician, a sportsperson or a social activist.

These people gain popularity through the way they create value in the world. We can debate how worthy that value is, but what's for certain is that, to their followers, those people are creating something worth paying attention to.

What they're not doing is staying quiet. They're creating something that is seen, heard, felt and appreciated. As fans and followers, we consume what they do.

Imagine a large art gallery. Thousands of people might come in and out each day. They've come to see the work of Da Vinci and the other old masters. The Da Vinci-watchers are the **consumers**. Each is essentially a faceless person in the crowd, but the gallery couldn't remain a going concern without them. The odd rich consumer might have their eye on a telephone auction where they could buy some of the work on the walls.

The curators and the other people who run the gallery help the artist's work be seen and appreciated. They talk about the work and give it the oxygen of exposure. Their presence gives the art a sense of place and authority, and it signals to the consumers that, yes, these are works worth talking about. These people are the **contributors**.

Finally, we've got the stars of the show. The artists whose work is up on the walls. These are the **creators**. Even though it's clear that they need the support of the contributors and consumers, they're the ones who are covered in the glory.

Few people go to a gallery because of the curator or their team. And no one goes because of the chance to brush shoulders with other viewers. It's the art and the artists being admired. The creators are the hub of value, and they're the ones who leave a legacy. This is the great thing about content: it can hang around and keep doing a job for its creator even when the creator is busy on whatever's next.

Now, I'm not going to coach you into thinking you're Da Vinci, but I am going to tell you that building content around the seed of a good idea could help that idea grow and create a sustainable business for you and for those you care about. Consider this bigger vision if your approach to date has been the rather less grand "let's just pay for some Facebook ads".

An often-cited 2006 report from the Nielsen Norman Group states that, "In most online communities, 90% of users are lurkers who never contribute, 9% of users contribute a little, and 1% of users account for almost all the action."[10]

More recent estimates suggest that the consumer group (the lurkers) may be smaller than 90% of all users. For example, in 2012, OnDigitalMarketing reported "spectator" figures of 73% in the US.[11] Whatever the true average figure is, there's no doubt that most people are consumers. That is to say, **the vast majority of online users are lurkers**.

On LinkedIn, for example, there are only 3 million content creators even though there are 260 million active users each month and more than 660 million users in total. Between them, those 3 million LinkedIn content creators mop up more than 9 billion impressions per week. (An impression is a measure of when a piece of content was loaded and could have been viewed.) These are big numbers and they're all being funnelled through the 1% of content creators.

From looking at my own stats on LinkedIn, I know that my contributor community is a tiny proportion of the people who view my content. I analysed 350 LinkedIn posts made between August 2018 and October 2019. Together, these posts racked up almost 1.7 million views. But only about 1.5% of those who viewed those posts clicked the like button, and only 0.7% added a comment (I've accounted for my own comments in response to other readers).

This shows that the huge majority of people who read my LinkedIn posts don't come out from behind the

---

10 https://www.nngroup.com/articles/participation-inequality/
11 https://ondigitalmarketing.com/learn/odm/research/
social-media-users/

velvet rope to reveal who they are. And yet I'm generally thought of as someone who gets good engagement. It's a consequence of the sheer number of people my content reaches. The percentage of contributors may be low but that still works out to be a lot of individuals.

Those contributors help me get results through my content. And that's the key point here: **the people who get results from content are the ones who create it**. While many more people are out there consuming that content, they're not the ones getting the true benefit from it. The creators take the glory.

As a service provider, I create content intended to speak directly to my ideal audience. Many of those people are in the consumer category. I'm not really conscious of them until the moment they "delurk" and announce that, yes, they've been following me for a while and are now ready to do business.

This can lead to a worrying thought, especially for the newer content creators out there. If you can't see or hear these lurkers, how do you really know they're there? What if you're just talking into the void and there's no one to receive your message? Put another way, what if the gallery's empty because no one's interested in your art? Is there any point in hanging another picture on the wall?

There are a couple of important points to note. The first is that it takes time to establish a meaningful and engaged audience.

Meaningful because you want to reach people who are relevant to your line of business. Anyone can reach an audience that isn't meaningful. Just pop off your clothes and run around the city centre. Someone will be live-streaming you on Twitter within a few minutes. This probably isn't the audience you want.

Engaged because it can take a while before people are ready to show you that they exist. When you first create content, no one will engage apart from the friends and family who've been pressured into leaving you the odd like.

As we saw when discussing the 30-month mindset, it really does take time to become known. You need to look for positive signals of progress to ensure that you stay on the right path and don't give up too soon. The lack of patience and grit are the enemies here. And remember: most overnight successes are years in the making.

From consumer to creator: the lurker's path to delurking

If you're in that majority group of consumer lurkers, you might want to think about how to break free of the crowd and get your paintings up on the gallery wall.

It's understandable that there are blockers in the way. Few people know who you are. You've never painted before. Putting your stuff up on a wall is scary and you'd rather run out of the room now before it all gets a bit too much.

The good news is that you don't have to go from zero to hero in one step. A lot of people who are now confident and regular content creators started out in the lurker group.

The simplest way to "delurk" is to start liking relevant content on social media. Likes are of very little value, so expect almost no one to notice this. That doesn't matter – to start is what matters. The next delurk action is only slightly more involved. It's spreading content by retweeting things on Twitter or sharing things on other platforms such as Facebook and LinkedIn. You can still do this with just a button click, but you're raising the stakes because now you're being more obvious in what you find appealing and relevant.

There's a tacit understanding on social media that you share the things you enjoy and find relevant and interesting. Don't believe the disclaimers that "retweet does not equal endorsement". Even if that's true for some individuals, this isn't how things are perceived by the people seeing those retweets.

The final stage is to move into the creator category – the zone of memorability, if you will. Remember that only 1% of all LinkedIn users are in that creator category[12] so being there will put you ahead of so many people in terms of your work being noticed and engaged with.

This doesn't mean you have to go nuts and try to emulate people who have a massive back-office content production arm propping them up. One or two posts per week is enough to get the ball rolling. The important thing is to say something valuable and to stick at it for long enough to build trust with a meaningful audience.

Unless you do both, content creation can be a time suck that doesn't return results. But do it right and it can be fabulous. My content has created the business I now have. It gets me clients directly and it also leads to referrals from my network. Let's look at referrals next.

---

12   https://kinsta.com/blog/linkedin-statistics/

20. REFERRALS: THE VALUE OF YOUR NETWORK

> Alone, we can do so little. Together,
> we can do so much.
> – Helen Keller

Get to the point

An engaged audience has the power to get your content in front of people who will buy from you. Connect with those in the "contributor" category and your content will have the best chance of being seen far and wide.

● ● ●

The most important people in your network will:

- **Engage with your content**, helping you get more visibility.
- **Refer you to clients**, helping you get more work.
- **Buy from you**, helping you keep a roof over your head.

Different people fall into different categories. The biggest category will be the "lurkers", who might not do any of the above, at least not at first. As we saw in the previous chapter, lurkers make up a large proportion of online user communities. My own stats show that the engagement rate on my LinkedIn content is less than 1% – that's a whole lot of people observing and not so many getting involved. You might have better success than me, but don't be surprised if the number of truly engaged people in your network is small.

Do what you can to build good relationships with those engaged people. The more you empower and appreciate your network, the more they'll help you. It's a virtuous circle. Remember that a big part of content success is in getting your material to be seen by others. One of my best LinkedIn tips is to ensure that you connect with everyone who comments with any substance on your posts or articles. You can apply this more generally to those who comment directly on your blog posts or who reply elsewhere on social media. These are the people in the contributor category who can help your content go places.

Sometimes, these people will be those we might traditionally see as our competitors. But in fact, they can be our biggest allies. This is how it's worked out for me in the copywriting field. There are loads of other people out there selling writing as a service. But through my Content DNA, I've come to be known as a trusted voice in the industry. My anchor value – relentlessly helpful – means that I do my best to help others whenever I can, and that includes those people who could potentially steal work from under my nose.

I go as far as to maintain a list of recommended copy-writers on my website,[13] so that potential clients have

---

13   https://espirian.co.uk/copywriters/

options in the event that I'm not the right person for them or that I'm just too busy to take on new work. This is the idea of being relentlessly helpful in action. Instead of giving some potential clients a flat "No, I can't do that" or "I'm too busy," I provide the helpful version of the response: "My colleague Victoria is an expert at that. Let me introduce you."

Whether you choose to see this as reciprocity, karma or pure madness is up to you. I've found that being community spirited works for me.

Instead of worrying about your competition, consider them to be in the contributor category. Get them onboard with your message to help your content spread far and wide. That's what will get you new clients. Those you might have seen as your competitors could truly become your messengers.

There's another important point here: although you should create content that's aimed at your ideal audience, it's fine to build a network that includes people who aren't part of that audience. Why? Because you can never be sure of which people *they* know. What matters is that you can build an engaged audience who are happy to help your content move organically through the social networks and on the web in general. A proportion of those people will recommend you to those they know who are a perfect fit for your products and services.

Through embracing this idea of building an engaged audience who are willing to say good things about me, I've earned countless referrals for my copywriting business. So, please don't worry too much if your content doesn't always get directly in front of your ideal customers. If the content is good enough, your audience will help it reach the right people. Referrals based on quality content are alive and well – and they can be the source of plenty of high-paying business.

All that said, it still makes sense to create content that's aimed at your ideal audience. Do you know who those people are? Let's take a look.

21. PEN PORTRAITS: YOUR IDEAL CUSTOMER

Personas are characters in your business story.
– Vicki O'Neill

Get to the point

Write down a detailed summary of who your ideal client is. All of your content and everything your business does will be in service of this imagined person.

● ● ●

One of the basics of marketing your business is to have a keen understanding of who your customer is, so that you can get to grips with what they want and how your product or service would be relevant in solving whatever problems they have.

At first blush, it's obvious that your business would be set up to serve the needs of your customers, and that to do anything else would mean putting your business at risk. After all, as management legend Peter Drucker once said, "The purpose of business is to create and keep a customer."

And yet, time and again, I speak to copywriting clients who don't have a sharp understanding of who they're serving. Their target market hasn't been defined beyond the base level of "We serve the people who pay us."

In the Content DNA world, this fuzziness isn't going to cut it. If you've defined the shape of your brand, you know what you stand for and what your key value proposition is. You should also be able to tune in to who your customers are and what they need and want from you.

This clarity on who the customer is comes from creating what I call a **pen portrait**. This isn't a literal picture but rather the characteristics that make that person who they are: their identity, circumstances, motivations, fears. In other circles, you'll hear this referred to as a customer avatar or buyer persona.

When you truly understand who this person is, you can write as though you were speaking directly to him or her. That leads to creating text that's more believable, more real.

Considerations when making a pen portrait

David Avrin, author of *Why Customers Leave (and How to Win Them Back)*, encourages us to ask several questions to help get in the heads of our customers:

- What do your customers dislike about doing business with your industry?
- What would they love if you could deliver it?
- What do they fear?
- What is their decision-making hierarchy in their business?
- What other choices do they have?

I've taken a couple of important lessons from David's work. The first relates to the final bullet point above: that our biggest competitor isn't other businesses but the *status quo*. For the average customer, doing nothing is easier than doing something. I've never been one to worry about competition, but I'd never really considered a potential customer's inaction to be the biggest blocker to my own business success. The message is clear: that we have to create an offering so tailored, distinctive and memorable that we become the top-of-mind option for our customers. I contend that it takes clear Content DNA, applied with consistency and congruence, to help us get to where the customer's urge to action beats their default state of inaction.

The second learning from David is an application of the Pareto principle, specifically that 20% of our customers make up 80% of our business. If we base our pen portraits on those 20% of customers, we'll create a template for who we most want to serve, safe in the knowledge that attracting such customers will bring us the most profits – and probably the fewest headaches.

A sample pen portrait

The imagined customers in my pen portraits are always named either Tony or Tina. Standard naming means I can ask my clients the same sorts of question: what would Tony think of this? Is this good for Tina? Would Tony buy X when he already bought Y last year?

Here's an example of a pen portrait for Tina, an imagined British customer for an online health-food store:

- 46 years old, married with two kids
- English home-owner and proud vegetarian
- Works part-time from home
- National Trust member
- Concerned about the environment

- University degree in English
- Not bothered about celebrity culture
- Can speak another language
- Prefers trains to cars
- Centre-left political views
- Not a fan of Brexit or of the royals
- Not as cool as her sister
- Rarely thinks about church
- Likes to volunteer at local events
- Thinks DIY isn't that hard
- Loves books (but not ebooks)
- Likes camping and UK holidays
- Prefers literary festivals to Glastonbury
- Prefers walks to paying for the gym
- Prefers glasses to contacts
- Listens to Radio 4 while gardening
- Enjoys red wine more than white
- Competent IT user but hates video games
- Secret disco music superfan

Sounds like a bit much? But say you were that online health-food store who had identified the lady above as the Tina for your business. If you were thinking about new product lines to bring on stream or strategic tie-ins with other businesses, do you think you'd have a feel for how she might react based on what's mapped out above?

Think of one of the most customer-centric businesses around: Amazon. Whatever your opinion of how they run their operation, there's no doubt that their core delivery service is one that millions of us trust and rely on, sometimes on a near-daily basis.

There have long been stories of Jeff Bezos, the big cheese at Amazon, insisting on leaving a seat empty at the table during board meetings. The message for everyone present couldn't be clearer: *for every business decision we make, we must keep the customer in mind.* If that's good enough for a multi-billion-dollar giant, it's probably good enough for us.

My list above only scratches the surface of what a pen portrait could be. As I want to practise what I preach, I've created my own pen portrait for my technical copywriting business. I use this as a showcase, so it's published on my website at espirian.co.uk/tony/.

By going into such detail about my Tony, I have a good handle on what his problems are and how I might be able to get rid of the hurdles he's facing. I can think of the things that might stop him from becoming a customer, and what might make him more loyal once he is a customer. And I can think about what language is best to make him feel as though he's in the right place when he sees content by me.

A big part of my job as a copywriter is to be an armchair psychologist. It's to work out what's burning my client's Tony or Tina right now and how to drown out the fire for them. You don't have to be a copywriter to take that same view in your business. You just have to appreciate the things that your customers struggle with and work to make their lives easier. This task becomes a whole lot easier if you can define who your own Tony or Tina is.

Evidence for the value of pen portraits

I wouldn't blame you if you're not dying to rush off and spend time creating a document about who your pen portrait is. But perhaps you'll be more inclined to do so when you see some of the evidence of the value of doing this exercise.

- Top-performing companies have mapped 90% or more of their customer database by pen portrait.[14]

- 56% of companies have developed higher quality leads using personas.[15]

- Website traffic increases 210% when using pen portraits, and pen portrait-based content increases customer engagement almost six times when targeting cold leads.[16]

You can create pen portraits yourself by following the advice in this chapter. Or you can save time by getting direct support from someone who does this sort of work for a living. Marketing and sales consultant Vicki O'Neill is the queen of personas and is my top pick in this category. If you need professional support in this area, check her out.[17] She also kindly contributed the data above about the value of pen portraits.

The best bit about having a pen portrait is that you'll always have a sounding board for your content. If you have a good enough idea of who your pen portrait is and what they care about, you'll be well placed to assess whether they're going to give a damn about the next blog post, video, podcast or whatever you put out.

If ever you suspect that your pen portrait would be put off by your content, then stop and think about whether your Content DNA is being represented in that content. If it is and your pen portrait still wouldn't like it, you've got a

---

14   https://www.cintell.net/17-high-performing-buyer-personas/

15   Itsma 2014: https://www.itsma.com/importance-of-developing-effective-personas/

16   Boardview 2015: https://boardview.io/blog/roi-case-study-how-personas-help-you-close-deals/

17   https://www.vickioneill.com/

decision to make: do you publish anyway and potentially alienate the people you're planning to work with? Or do you adjust who your pen portrait is?

Your Content DNA should help you create an attractive shape for your pen portrait. If your Content DNA and pen portrait definitions don't overlap strongly, you're unlikely to work with people who love what you do and tell others about it.

As Mark Schaefer puts it in *Marketing Rebellion*, "The best companies are fans of their fans." You're much more likely to enter a mutual fan relationship if you can first identify with each other.

The other big benefit of writing with your pen portrait in mind is that your content can be framed as though it's part of a conversation with a single person. If you want to use conversational, human language in your copy, this is a great way to do it.

Sample questions for building your own pen portrait

Let's get the ball rolling and create a pen portrait. Once you start this exercise, you should find that you can think of lots of other preferences to fill in for your pen portrait.

Don't limit yourself: the more detail, the better. Something that may seem irrelevant now might be useful in informing your thinking later on.

- Name, age, location (the basics).
- Employment type, role and seniority.
- Financial security and status in life.
- Personality type (introverted, extroverted).
- Politics, beliefs and views about societal issues.
- Hobbies, likes and dislikes.
- Attitudes toward risk, change and innovation.

- Problems and concerns.
- Future plans and hopes.

The big mistake with pen portraits

There's no doubt that pen portraits are useful in helping us find the right way of speaking to our customers. But here's the thing: it's not good to be too wedded to your pen portrait. Why? Because sometimes you will be approached by clients who don't fit the profile of your pen portrait. In your well-meaning belief that you need to serve a particular type of customer and only that type of customer, you might turn away perfectly good business.

Now, that's fine if you have a queue of people stretching around the corner, all desperate to give you money. But that's not how things are for most businesses.

For my own pen portrait, Tony's business installs custom metal pipes and parts. Does that mean that I should provide technical writing only to other businesses that install the same pipes? Of course not. Tony also likes to wear an England rugby shirt. Does that mean I can serve only England fans? No, that would be stupid. I have permission to serve people who are not like my pen portrait. And so do you.

Think of your pen portrait as the centre of a dartboard of potential customers. You need to have something to aim at, but if you don't hit a bullseye then there are still plenty of scoring options on the board.

We also need to be wary of pigeonholing people too much. High-level data alone would put Prince Charles and Ozzy Osbourne in the same group.[18] They are the same age and share many other characteristics. And yet they're

---

18   https://www.bbc.co.uk/news/technology-37307829

totally different princes. One of them is an evil prince of darkness! You can fill in the rest of that joke.

So there: don't become a slave to your pen portrait. It should guide you, but it's not everything. Focusing on your own Content DNA will mean that your brand values naturally attract the sort of people who want to work with you.

The celebrity shortcut

If building a pen portrait isn't for you but you feel as though you have a decent idea of what your ideal customer likes, try this shortcut: think of which celebrity would most appeal to your target audience. It's the same idea as the celebrity voice method I mentioned earlier for coming up with your own Content DNA.

If you have someone in mind, imagine what they would say when talking to your ideal customer. If you can produce content that the reader feels is familiar and identifiable, you have the makings of an effective business writing style.

I'm not suggesting that you abandon your own writing "voice" in favour of the chosen celebrity. But think about the opportunities to bring in some styles that would appeal to the audience without losing the essence of what you want to say.

Whichever means you use to craft a pen portrait of your imagined ideal customer, try to keep it to hand, especially if you're new to creating content or if your previous content hasn't been getting you any results. Next time you're at the keyboard, remember to ask yourself whether your Tony or Tina will like what you're putting out. The more you ask yourself that question, the more in tune you'll be with what your real customers want and need from you.

Of course, it's all well and good to know who you want to serve. But what about the people you *don't* want to serve? It's time to check out the pen portrait's evil twin.

22. POISON PORTRAITS: THE SALESY DOUCHE CANOE

Marketing can be a filter as well as a magnet.
– Doug Kessler

Get to the point

Have a clear idea of who you don't want to serve. Make sure that your content and processes actively repel those people, so that you can focus on the clients who energise you.

● ● ●

Your pen portrait is that picture of the ideal audience member: the person you most want to influence to do business with you. As valuable as it is to have a clear idea of who you want to serve, there's a complement to this that is often ignored or overlooked.

Inspired by a talk by my marketing buddies Andrew and Pete, I came up with a name for the evil twin version of a pen portrait. I call it a poison portrait.

Your poison portrait is the imagined person who you *don't* want to deal with in your business. Your content and entire approach to business should consciously repel them from your door.

I characterise my poison portrait as being a salesy

douche canoe. I haven't defined him (of course it's a him) in the same detail as I have with my Tony, but I know him well enough to spot him from a long way off.

My salesy douche canoe is a "me, me, me" ass who would do anything to make a sale. He has slicked-back hair, an awful fake tan and an oversized gold watch. He turns up late to everything and always thinks his opinion is the most important. You can probably piece together the rest.

He'd definitely be put off hiring a service provider who wears a T-shirt to meetings or who puts cartoons into his keynote presentations. In short, he's never going to be bothering my inbox, and that's good for my sanity.

You need to be a little brave if you decide not to serve your poison portrait. Doing so means leaving money on the table, and that can be hard to justify to yourself and your family. But trust me: this is the smart long-term play. The fewer headaches you have in your business, the happier and more successful you'll be.

Remember that your business doesn't have to appeal to everyone. If your Content DNA defines an interesting shape, it's natural that some people just won't like it – that's a good thing. You're not here to serve those people. The more you can filter them out of your pipeline, the more time and energy you'll have to focus on those who do like what you do.

Here's why you should have a clear picture of your poison portrait:

- It's easy.
- It's fun.
- It keeps you alert to red flags.
- It helps you understand your pen portrait.

Why ... it's easy

It can be hard to put your finger on something you like, but it's much simpler to identify what you can't stand. If you're in an ice cream shop and there are 200 flavours, it might be tough to choose your favourite. What if you haven't checked all the options? What if you make the wrong choice? But you can much more easily rule out what you can't stand.

Why ... it's fun

It can be scary to think creatively but in this case you can relieve some tension by going to town and imagining all the things you'd hate when dealing with a real customer. Roll up every bad business transaction, terrible date and whatever else you can conjure up. Let it all out.

Why ... you avoid red flags

Success comes from taking the actions that lead you towards your desired goal. That starts with thinking positively and intentionally about what you want and what you're going to do to make it happen. This is why sports psychologists get football players to mentally rehearse actions such as taking and scoring a penalty kick.

Having a good idea of what you don't want can be the useful flip side of this. For some people, chasing a goal is easier to achieve when you're also running away from a wolf.

The pain of dealing with terrible customers is something you should want to avoid. Describing the shape of that terrible customer means you're better placed to sidestep them when the time comes.

When you write your poison portrait, think about the signs and language used when someone is about to become a bad customer. The sooner you can dodge that person, the less stress you'll have.

Writing this down makes you more tuned to spot potential bad customers who turn up in your inbox and elsewhere in life. Put another way: invite the wrong guests and your party is going to suck hard.

When you become well known in your industry, you may be able to avoid the poison portrait as soon as they give you the merest glimpse that they might not be a perfect fit for you. Until then, you'll probably need to give them more rope before you make a judgement on how douchey their canoe is.

Why ... you appreciate your pen portraits

Even if you've written a good pen portrait, there's probably a fair chance that you could improve it. Understanding who you don't want to serve will help you sharpen your definition of who you do want to serve.

Remember that your ideal customer is your fan. Your job is to be their fan and to give them an experience so great that they can't wait to tell their friends, family and co-workers how awesome it was to buy from you.

Now do this:

Write a profile of your imagined poison portrait.
You could base this on your worst actual customer, but unless they were a total nightmare then you can probably imagine someone even worse than that.

Here are some ideas:

- They think it's OK to call you late on Sunday evening (because they're just back from Dubai and why can't you be flexible?).

- They want your product or service at half price or even free (because that Audi TT isn't paying for itself).

- They want you to go to their office so they can keep you waiting, mess you around with their aggressive dogs and subject you to lots of swearing and terrible coffee. And then not give you the project (because ... well, there is no "because", because they've ghosted you).

You'll be able to come up with lots of these, I'm sure. And the things that annoy you will probably differ from those that annoy me. Please have fun with this. Life is hard and you probably have a million things on your plate besides reading this book.

So, we've seen who you do and don't want to appeal to in your content. But what should you create content about? Let's find out.

23. WHAT TO WRITE ABOUT AND HOW TO FIND CONTENT IDEAS

No matter what people tell you, words and ideas can change the world.
– Robin Williams

Get to the point

You should never run out of content ideas if you know your customers well enough. Think about the real questions they ask and how you could answer them at scale.

● ● ●

There's an old saying that goes, "If you want to understand something, try to teach it." If you want your core business offering to improve, create content about it. But *what* content should you create? This is the question I hear most often from people who are struggling to get started.

For me, this comes back to understanding your customers well enough. If you have a sharp idea of who your Tony or Tina is, you should know what their headaches are. You should also understand how your product or service can make their life better.

In a nutshell, your content needs to exhibit the shape of your Content DNA while providing helpful information that addresses your customers' problems, queries and concerns.

The basics of content marketing

The following categories form the basis of the content marketing strategy set out in Marcus Sheridan's book, *They Ask, You Answer*. They're a great place to start if you want to create content that genuinely helps your ideal audience.

- **Price**: how much does a product or service cost, and what factors influence the price?
- **Problems**: what are the objections to someone becoming a customer?
- **Reviews**: what relevant products and services can be objectively reviewed?
- **Comparisons**: how does one product, service or package compare with another?
- **Best of**: what are the best-in-class products and services in an industry?
- **How to**: how do you complete step-by-step processes?

Content around these topics is popular. Think about it: when you're looking to hire a service provider, I bet that "How much does it cost?" is near the top of your list of questions.

And if you're looking for trust signals, you're bound to seek out reviews. And if you're trying to fix a technical problem, you might look for a walkthrough.

Stages of problem awareness

Your potential clients may need all sorts of different content from you depending on where they are on the scale of awareness. This measures how aware they are of whatever problem is causing them pain.

When I talk to copywriting clients, I ask them to think about what figurative pain it is that they take away from their customers. Drilling into that is often the key to creating an effective message that makes people want to buy.

This point about pain and the awareness of it means that there's a lot of content needed to cover all bases. For example, someone's pain (if we can agree to call it that) might be that they can't stream video through their upstairs computer.

Now, this person might be at a relatively low level of awareness of the problem. They know something's not right but have no idea about the cause or about ways to fix it. At the other end of the spectrum, another person in the same situation might be at the point of fixing their streaming pain by choosing a product.

They've already done research to show that their internet setup is fine, but have discovered that the thick walls in their house mean that the Wi-Fi signal isn't strong upstairs. They've also found out that Wi-Fi isn't the only possible internet solution, and that they can use their home's electrical circuits to carry the signal to other parts of the building. Furthermore, they know of providers who make such equipment and now they just need to make a comparison of hardware options before making a purchase.

If you imagine someone moving through these stages of awareness, you'll realise that they ask different questions at each stage and that they need relevant content that answers those questions at each stage.

An early-stage question might be "Why can't I stream Netflix?" but a late-stage question might be "Product X technical specifications". Both bits of content will be useful, but at different times.

The point is that you can't predict the stage of awareness your potential customers will have. So, you need to create content that serves them at all stages, from the "something's annoying me" stage through to the "I know exactly what I need and now I'm checking specs and prices" stage.

(By the way, you really can use your home's electrical circuits to carry your internet signal from your broadband router to other parts of the house. The devices needed for this use a technology often referred to as "powerline". One of the common powerline standards is called "HomePlug". I've been using HomePlug to juice up my home office for years. It still feels a bit like magic.)

This is all the sort of stuff we expect to be able to find answers to when we search the web about any topic. Are any potential customers wondering about such things in your industry? Of course they are. The question is, do you want to let others provide the answers? Or would it be better for you to be the answer-giver? If you were searching for information, would you be more likely to trust a business that was giving helpful answers to questions, or would you prefer a business that stayed silent?

The goldmine of email

Your email inbox and sent items folders are great places to understand what questions your clients are asking you and what answers you might be able to provide at scale.

Take those one-to-one conversations, remove the personal information and publish the content. That way, you can have a conversation at scale with countless potential customers online.

I put a lot of store in "asking the audience". Without doing this, content can become a bit too insular. You just can't serve people well unless you talk with them, and not enough people take time to understand what their audience wants. Be the exception: talk with your customers, find out what questions they have and then answer them at scale.

Your email inbox and sent items folders are a goldmine of those questions and answers. So get digging.

Andy Crestodina is a content marketing hero of mine. Here's his approach to question mining:

- A customer emails you a question.
- You reply in detail, giving that person an amazingly comprehensive answer.
- You turn that epic answer into content for your site.
- Another customer asks you the same question.
- You point them to your ready-made content, and add any extra context that's relevant to them.

This takes effort but it also leads to some nice wins:

Win 1

The first customer comes away from this interaction thinking about how you went above and beyond in answering their email. They might have expected an automated reply asking them to trawl through some FAQs. Instead, a human replied with a proper response that gave them everything they needed.

Win 2

The second customer should also feel good about their interaction with you. Their question is validated by the fact that you've already prepared a good answer. If you can give people that "here's one I prepared earlier" feeling when you answer their questions through ready-made content, they'll be more apt to trust you.

Why? Because you've signalled to them that yours is the sort of business that provides helpful answers to real questions. And where are they going to turn next time they need help? To your website.

Win 3

Aside from looking great, you'll save yourself a lot of hassle with this approach. Instead of expending the time and mental energy to answer every question individually, you set yourself up to answer at scale and make yourself look more authoritative in doing so. And your long-term support burden will decrease.

If you have staff answering your customers' emails, giving them the instruction to provide a detailed response and then to earmark that information for publication on your website is the smart way to build a content footprint that serves your customers' needs.

Document your sales process

What things do you explain to people on sales calls and in meetings?

If you could set that out in a bunch of articles, it would help your potential customers and make your life easier. By writing down the info that you share in your sales meetings, you'll naturally become better at explaining those same things when you're face to face with people.

This kind of information is what customers need to know but might not yet be educated enough to realise they need to know it.

Customers who research you before you try to sell to them will then know the process, and this should take the stress out of any sales calls as well as speeding things up.

Here are some examples to get you thinking, depending on your business:

- How long does delivery take?
- What are the lead times?
- How do you handle free trials?
- What is the warranty period?
- What questions do you need to ask the customer on a sales call?

Think about customer obstacles

Your content should help to address your customers' fears and concerns. Ask yourself what might stop your ideal client buying from you. Eventually, you should reach the stage where you've published so much relevant content that any objections will be easy to overcome.

Here are some common objections you can overcome through your content:

- **It's too expensive**: talk about the factors that determine your price.
- **Don't know how product/service will help**: create content that shows the problems you solve.
- **What if something goes wrong?**: address misconceptions and talk about how you support customers.

- **Perhaps there's something better elsewhere**: make comparisons with alternative options.

Why does this work? Because when you knock all of the hurdles out of the way, your prospective customer is more likely to say yes to trying your product or service.

Read any book on how the brain works and you'll know that people make decisions emotionally, not rationally. Just because a prospective customer has no rational objection to doing business with you, that's no guarantee that they *will* do business with you. Still, clearing their path of hurdles is a good move. Make your business the easy choice.

Research gaps in your industry

It's easy to think that everything has already been written about. But consider this: have you ever searched Google and found an answer that wasn't exactly what you wanted? What if one of your clients was searching for an answer and didn't find exactly what they wanted? Is there a gap that your content could fill?

Put yourself in your customers' shoes and try to do some searches for the kinds of things they might be looking for. How good is the information you find on the web? Analyse the results and ask yourself some questions:

- Is the content clear?
- Are all the facts right?
- Would the content make you (the pretend customer) confident to buy? If not, why?
- Has anything been missed out?
- What hasn't been done well?

Good content isn't just about what you say. It's also about how you say it. I create a lot of content and almost all of it has been covered before. What's different is my tone of voice, my personality. Pour your own chilli sauce over your content and make it your own. (I always end up talking about food.)

Make a note of what you type in when you search for content topics you could write about. Does your own website or blog appear in the search results? If not, could you write some content that provides a good answer to the thing you searched for?

This concept of looking up the words and phrases that customers might be searching for and seeing what content is already out there is called **keyword research**. In this context, a keyword often means a phrase (more than one word).

Keywords are the terms you want to include in your own content so that search engines can help your audience find your stuff.

As Andy Crestodina sets out in *Content Chemistry*, your ideal keywords meet three criteria:

1. **Good search volume**: people should be searching for the keyword. If no one's searching for a keyword, there's little value in ranking for it.

2. **Low competition**: your website has a realistic chance of ranking for the keyword when compared with the other websites out there trying to do the same. An uncontested space is the easiest place to dominate.

3. **High relevance**: the keyword should align with what your business is about. Ranking for irrelevant words won't help you build authority in your niche. But ranking for highly relevant keywords means that both the search engines and real people will have a clear idea of what you're all about.

Those are the ingredients for a good keyword. But how do you find the right keywords for your business?

That's where some handy free search tools come in. Check these out:

- **KWFinder**: my favourite keyword lookup tool, which offers two free lookups per day. See also the related tools SERPChecker and SERPWatcher by the same company (Mangools).

- **Keywords Everywhere**: free web browser plugin to display keyword search data on Google search results page.

- **Keyword Tool**: free keyword lookup tool.

- **Google autocomplete**: start typing a search related to your business and see what Google suggests in the dropdown menu.

- **Google related searches**: when a search is complete, look at the list of suggestions at the bottom of the page.

- **Answer The Public**: enter a topic or industry and see what related questions are shown.

- **Quora**: search for relevant topics and see what questions are being asked and answered.

- **Amazon reviews**: good for checking customers' phrasing and understanding their frustrations.

Own a geographical niche

If your product or service is relevant only to a particular region, you can strengthen your chances of being found by adding your location to the keywords you want to rank for.

Let's say that the previous tip helped you find keywords such as these:

Freelance marketing consultant

If you wanted local clients, you might tweak this to:

Freelance marketing consultant in Birmingham

There might be a lot of competition from people who base their content around the first keyword. There will be a lot less for the second.

And while the second keyword will naturally be searched much less often than the first, anyone who does search for the second keyword will have a much higher chance of clicking through to your site and ultimately doing business with you.

Even if the location of your business isn't relevant (for example, you make products that could be shipped anywhere or you provide a service that could be delivered online), it doesn't hurt to add your location to your content so that people who want to buy from or hire a local person can do so.

This speaks to a funny quirk of psychology. Even though we're often happy to search for service providers online and communicate with them remotely via chat messages, video calls, emails and telephone conversations, we still feel better in the knowledge that someone is local.

That's despite the fact that we might have no need ever to meet them.

Engage your creative side

All of the above is based on method and logic. It'll be enough to cover a lot of the bases in creating content that helps to educate your audience and support them to make better buying decisions.

This sort of formulaic approach suits some better than others. But if you're more of a creative thinker, perhaps the following will be a better fit.

Use a distraction activity

Give your brain a break and get away from the screen. I don't really believe in fate or the universe being playful with us, but it's funny how all my best ideas arrive while I'm in the shower, out of reach of any note-taking apparatus. I'm one of the cleanest copywriters on the circuit.

Turn a sentence into a short story

This one's simple but powerful: pick a book (fiction works best for this) and select a sentence anywhere in it. Then spend a few minutes constructing a short story based on that sentence. I did this once while squirrelled away on a copywriting retreat. It's good for unblocking the mind and getting you back into your flow.

Do some word association

This classic method lets your mind run free:

- Think of a word (related to your business or not).
- What's the next word that comes to mind? And the next?

- Construct a chain of words by thinking only about the previous word.

- Try it for a minute or so, ideally saying the words out loud. If you want to capture the process, do it in a voice memo.

Once you're done, consider the chain of words. You shouldn't have thought too deeply about any particular link in the chain, but the whole sequence together might make for an interesting examination of what's in your head. What further ideas does it give you?

Think of alternative uses for an everyday object

What fun can you have imagining how to use the boring and the commonplace items all around you?

A brick is the classic example for this activity. Here's what I came up with:

- Hide-and-seek zone for fairies.
- Ping-pong-ball holder.
- Raised plate in case of table floods.
- Strongman juggling equipment.
- World's worst percussion instrument.
- Donald Trump skin-tone matcher.

This all seems silly but it gets you to look at things from a different angle. And it really is good exercise for your mind. If we think of the brain as a muscle that needs a regular workout, this sort of thing could be your equivalent of squats and lunges. (Real gyms are a distant memory for me.)

Let's move on and look at the importance of applying congruence to your visuals. That's right: a writer trying to tell you about graphics. Will wonders never cease?

24. BE VISUALLY CONSISTENT

No one is an artist unless he carries his picture in his head before painting it, and is sure of his method and composition.

– Claude Monet

Get to the point

Beautifully crafted words sparkle less if they're surrounded by inconsistent visuals. Stand out in the social feed by ensuring that your static and moving images are recognisably you.

● ● ●

My day job is to put consonants and vowels in the right order. But more than that, it's to communicate clearly so that the target audience understands how stuff works. Communication is the journey of ideas and feelings from one brain to another. Words and visuals are co-pilots on the flight. They work best when they complement each other. So, even though I'm a writer, I recognise the value of adding the right visuals to the mix.

It's all too easy to grab some photos from one of the numerous free stock image websites, chuck them into Canva (a free image composition website), then share the results on your social media feeds or your website. It feels as though you're doing something to liven up your content and perhaps get more engagement.

Except that this sort of visual curation is at best painting a fuzzy shape of your brand. You should instead want to draw clear and sharp lines – metaphorically, at least. Now, I'm not a designer. That's why I've had my logo, book cover and website professionally designed. If I did it myself, it would take ages and would still end up looking homemade.

But despite not being a graphics wizard, I've learned a couple of useful skills over the years. The first is being able to appreciate which visuals stand out in social feeds and in general web searches. The second is knowing what doesn't work and understanding why I don't like it.

What I've found is that the visuals that always stick in my head are characterised by a few things:

- **It's always clear where the image came from**. The logo or some other identifier grounds me in what I'm looking at.

- **There are never more than three main colours**. (White, grey and black get a free pass with me.)

- **Positions, sizes and typefaces are always consistent**. If you use 14pt Times New Roman in one image and 20pt Helvetica in another, have a coffee and feel my silent judgement.

Images that have a consistent look and feel will be easily recognised when they're shared on social media. They get people's attention and jog their memory even if they don't stop to read the content.

When I started using a Bitmoji cartoon of myself (I call him BitmoJohn) in my blogs in 2017, my social shares started to be noticed more. Was my content any better? Probably not. But this cartoon had given a distinct visual identity to my social shares. Licensing issues mean that I can't include BitmoJohn in this book. The irony of telling people to be congruent and then not being fully able to execute on that myself isn't lost on me.

The lesson I learned from my Bitmoji experience is to be sure that you own the assets from which your brand identity is built. So, I encourage you to get your own photos taken and your own custom image templates designed. Be in control of your visual brand so that every piece of content you put out has a consistent look to it.

Yes, there's a cost to all this. As well as paying a designer for new designs, I had to pay virtual assistants to go and apply those new designs to all of my existing content. And on top of that, there's the ongoing effort to ensure that any future content I put out is in line with everything else. This last bit isn't too onerous for me, because, once I get used to a task, it soon becomes second nature.

If you want to move beyond a free tool such as Canva but don't want to dive into the potential complexity of Photoshop, a great in-between option is Snagit by TechSmith. For only ~£50, it's a fab screenshot and image composition tool for Windows and Mac. Almost all the graphics you see from me are made using Snagit.

A 2019 study of more than 300 bloggers[19] found that 43% of them were using four or more images per blog post. I'm in that bracket, too, and am making my content more visually compelling all the time.

The same 2019 study reported on how long it took bloggers to create the visuals for their blog posts:

---

19   https://blog.bannersnack.com/visual-anatomy-of-a-blog-post/

- 62%: up to an hour.
- 28%: between one and three hours.
- 9%: more than three hours.

It's difficult to be prescriptive here. Prepping images for a highly technical blog with complex flowcharts and annotated wireframes of engine designs is clearly going to take a lot longer than processing photos for a lifestyle blog that reveals which superfoods are hot this month.

Where you can, use branded templates. If image creation isn't what you're good at, outsource the task to someone who can do the job better, faster and cheaper than you can. Above all, don't let crappy, inconsistent images weaken your brand identity. Maintain the right shape everywhere.

Create videos

Videos are the big brother of visuals, and they build a bridge with your audience better than just about any other medium. (There's a strong argument for the "in your ear" intimacy of audio podcasts being the best way to connect with your audience, but that's a debate for another time.)

Think of ways to be consistent and congruent in all your videos. That means:

- Wearing clothing that suits your personal brand.
- Recording in the same spot, with the same lighting.
- Using standard thumbnail images (the initial image frames that help with promotion).

Traditional landscape video (an aspect ratio of 16:9) is fine if you're going to host your videos on YouTube or Vimeo and then share that content on your website.

If you intend to share videos on social media, square format (for the maths fans, that's a 1:1 aspect ratio) tends to work best. Why? Because square videos take up 78% more space in social feeds than landscape videos do.

To borrow a phrase from social media scheduling company Buffer, this means that square videos have more "thumb-stopping power" on social media.

If you create "talking-head" video on mobile, I recommend Apple Clips for iOS. Not only is it free but also it creates square video automatically, making it perfect for social media. And on top of that, it even adds on-the-fly captions (subtitles).

If your videos are more involved than simple talking-head content shot on mobile, there's some work to do to produce square video output. For example, you could create a square template in a program such as Camtasia by TechSmith, or use a number of other tools to edit your video into shape.

If you want to avoid the technical hassle of getting this right, a great option is to record your video however you're able to and then send it to a human-powered production service such as Splasheo (go to splasheo.com/john to try it for free).

Splasheo offer lots of ready-made templates to choose from, and you can select your colours, logo and other settings before letting the team do the work to create the final video. The service also includes embedded captions, so it's ideal if you have a small marketing budget and want one less headache.

Now, I've developed the techie skills to be able to do my own square videos, but I still use done-for-you services like these because they help me claw back time in my busy schedule.

(This isn't a book about productivity but, in a nutshell, it's a good idea to look at all the tasks you do in a week and then work out what you can eliminate or delegate. Whatever's left behind ought to be the high-value work that drives your business forward. Get everything else out of your head and off your shoulders. If you don't do this, your business either won't grow at the rate you'd like it to or it will grow and then you'll have a nervous breakdown. You decide.)

Anyway, look at my social videos and you'll see consistent brand colours, progress bars, fonts and logos. It's all about being the right shape.

I don't finish my social videos with the usual needy begging for viewers to like and subscribe. As a bit of fun and to do something a little more memorable, I instead end with my logo, a positive chime sound and my daughter's voice saying "relentlessly helpful technical copywriting by my dad". It's my cheeky geek Content DNA building block in action.

Caption this

If you make the leap to creating videos, it's essential to include captions. The stats tell the story:

In 2016, Digiday reported that 85% of Facebook video is watched without sound.[20]

In 2018, an official LinkedIn article[21] stated that: "The vast majority (80%) of video views on LinkedIn take place with the sound off. It's hardly surprising therefore that video content designed for silent

---

20   https://digiday.com/media/silent-world-facebook-video/
21   https://business.linkedin.com/en-uk/marketing-solutions/blog/
     posts/B2B-video/2018/Ready-to-get-started-with-video-ads-on-
     LinkedIn-Here-are-9-things-you-need-to-know

viewing is 70% more likely to be watched all the way through to the end."

A small study by Instapage[22] of 16.5 hours of Facebook videos showed that:

- The average reach of a captioned video was 16% higher than the same video without captions.
- Reactions to captioned videos were 17% higher on average than they were for the same uncaptioned video.
- Average shares dropped by nearly 15% when captions were removed.
- Clicks of CTA buttons fell by 26% when captions were removed.

Verizon Media and Publicis Media's 2019 survey of 5616 US consumers[23] found that:

- 69% of respondents view video with sound off in public places.
- 80% of respondents said they were more likely to watch an entire video when captions were available.

Captions aren't just good for accessibility and visibility. Research by AdColony and Millward Brown[24] shows that captions can increase brand awareness by 18.8%. So, you'll

---

22 https://instapage.com/blog/closed-captioning-mute-videos
23 https://www.3playmedia.com/2019/07/19/verizon-media-and-publicis-media-find-viewers-want-captions/
24 https://adtechdaily.com/2017/01/26/subtitling-adverts-can-help-increase-brand-awareness/

have a better chance of making people watch your content and remember your brand if your videos contain captions.

Here are some good use cases for adding captions to videos. Consider that people consuming your content:

- are in a shared space and can't turn the sound on.
- are deaf or hard of hearing.
- are unable to understand the speaker's accent.
- are not native English speakers.

Even if none of the above applies, captions give a more polished, professional look to a video – and that could serve to keep people engaged and increase the time they spend watching your content.

There are a huge number of apps and services for producing video captions. I've already mentioned Apple Clips as a free and fully mobile option and Splasheo[25] if you want help with the video production and captioning together. Another great option is Rev[26], which produces plain-text captions files (called SRT files) that you upload on social media to accompany your original video files.

Other popular captioning services include Kapwing and QuiCC. In short, there are lots of options that suit all sorts of video workflows. Whichever method you choose, make sure that your videos are captioned.

It's worth knowing about the two different types of captions:

- **Open captions** are "burned in" to the video file, which means they're always visible. The viewer has no choice whether or not to see the captions.

---

25 https://www.splasheo.com
26 bit.ly/captions10

The text can't be read by search engines, but the look and feel is under the full control of the creator, which can reinforce their visual brand.

- **Closed captions** are not part of the video file. They're uploaded as a separate file (usually in SRT format) along with the video. They're optional and the viewer can turn them on or off using controls on the video. Because the captions are included as discrete text files, they can be inspected by search engines, and that makes them good for search engine optimisation (SEO).

From the congruence point of view, I like open captions because they give you control over exactly what the audience sees. If I want to use a typeface that matches what I use on my website (and I do!), that's something I can do only if I use open captions. On the other hand, closed captions are good if you want to give people a choice, and they tend to have quite a standard look about them. You have to choose what's right for you.

Bonus tip to improve the visibility of your videos: Meryl Evans, my digital marketing buddy and long-time captions advocate, recommends tagging social media video posts with the hashtag #captioned. This indicates that such video content contains captions, and can aid the discoverability of that content by people who are looking for accessible videos.

OK, that's enough about visuals. Let's think a bit about something that gets many creatives excited: naming.

25. GET YOUR NAMING RIGHT

Lisa: A rose by any other name would
smell as sweet.

Bart: Not if you called 'em stench blossoms.

– The Simpsons

Get to the point

Giving names to services and ideas gives those things more significance and makes them easier to refer to and remember. Create names that fit your brand and use them consistently.

● ● ●

Defining your own language is a powerful way to take control of the way you communicate. Your own words and phrases become your calling cards – the things that, when seen and spoken, are the shortcuts to remind people that you exist and that you offer something different.

In *Clarity Wins*, Steve Woodruff expands on this idea. He ditches traditional expressions in favour of his own catchier alternatives. We'll hear more from Steve in chapter 31 (The Content DNA interviews).

Hashtags

Hashtags are the words and phrases used to help categorise and search for content on social media. Having your own branded hashtag could help your business stand out and provide an easy way for followers to spread the word about you.

Big businesses use their own hashtags to help with brand recognition and cross-platform advertising. But you don't have to be Nike or McDonald's to do the same thing. Come up with a good idea and you can nab yourself a hashtag for free.

Top tips for creating good hashtags

- **Choose a unique name**: if the hashtag you want to use has already been used, it's not a good idea to try to reuse it for your own purposes.

- **Choose a short name**: short hashtags usually work best (long hashtags are better for humorous one-offs).

- **Don't use punctuation**: hashtags can be made up of letters and numbers only. Grammar nerds may moan at you but you can tell them that punctuation simply isn't supported by hashtags.

- **Make it memorable**: use rhymes or alliteration to give your hashtag some rhythm and flow. For example, I use #NoPainerExplainer (which rhymes) and #LinkedInLearnerLounge (which uses alliteration, where each word starts with the same letter).

- **Capitalise each word**: hashtags aren't case sensitive but are often easier to read when each word is capitalised, for example #UnclogYourBlog versus #unclogyourblog.

There's a special term for writing capitals inside a squashed-together phrase such as UnclogYourBlog. It's called CamelCase because the caps look like the humps of a camel. It's good for screen readers, which makes it a win for accessibility.

Once you have a name in mind, search for it across the social networks. The perfect scenario is to find zero results. If the hashtag hasn't been used before, that means you can use it yourself.

For my business, I've created hashtags for a few different activities, including #LinkedInLearnerLounge and #UnclogYourBlog. Developing my own branded language is a way for me to stand out from other copywriters. You can do the same, no matter what business you're in. For example, marketing expert Janine Coombes uses #SecretMarketingShow for her funny video series of marketing tips on LinkedIn and YouTube.

Once you have a hashtag that you like and that isn't being used by anyone else, start using it. That's how you go about associating the hashtag with you and your account. What you don't want is to think of a cool hashtag and then *not* use it straightaway. That gives people licence to swoop in and use it for themselves.

Add the hashtag to your social media profiles. This means that when people search for the hashtag, they will also see your account at the top of the search results.

Hashtags are not case-sensitive. This means that #contentdna is treated the same as #ContentDNA (which is the version that smart people use when using social media to mention this book).

However, it's good to use capitals at the start of each word. This helps with readability and accessibility, meaning that hashtags are easier for humans and screen readers to understand when they include capitals.

Without the capitals, you might read the words incorrectly. Think about the Italian division of the energy company Powergen and then compare the hashtag #PowergenItalia with #PowerGenitalia (ouch). Or how about the hashtag for Susan Boyle's album launch: compare #SusanAlbumParty with #SusAnalBumParty (peachy).

There's no formal way to register a hashtag, so it isn't the same as a social media username, which you *do* have to register.

With hashtags, you use your imagination to come up with a name that no one else is using. If you have an idea for a hashtag and can see that it hasn't been used before, you can simply start adding it to your posts. Before long, it'll be seen as yours. Well, sort of ...

Because the hashtag isn't registered, you can't truly consider it to be yours. If a competitor with a much more engaged following started using it after you, that might drown out your use of the hashtag, and you might have to look elsewhere.

Of course, that's not a nice thing for them to do, and if they were responsible, they would have searched for the hashtag, seen you were already using it and left it well alone. Sometimes branded hashtags will be hijacked and reused by porn/spam accounts. Sadly, apart from blocking the accounts in question, you can't do anything to stop such inappropriate posts being made.

Bad hashtag practice

People sometimes use popular hashtags that are nothing to do with their post just so that their content can get more visibility.

For example, #haro (short for Help A Reporter Out) and #journorequest are meant to be used by journalists to help them gather information for their stories. But they're often used by people who are looking for more attention on their posts. Don't do this. And if you're not sure what a hashtag is for, don't use it.

A tip for event hashtags on Twitter

If you're attending an event, add the event's hashtag to your profile. Anyone looking for that event may then see your profile. It usually takes Twitter several hours to update so that search results reflect these changes, so I recommend updating your profile at least 24 hours before the event.

The approach doesn't work well if lots of people have the same hashtag in their profile, and this is particularly true if the hashtag doesn't relate to a specific event. For example, don't expect that adding #SEO to your profile will have any effect on your visibility in search results.

As well as being a useful personal branding tool, hashtags play an extra role on LinkedIn. They help you find "untagged" shares of your content.

By "untagged", I mean LinkedIn posts of yours that someone else has shared without mentioning you in their post. If you use a branded hashtag in your original post, then searches on that hashtag should reveal shares that others have made on that post.

To save time, bookmark your LinkedIn hashtag searches to quickly check who's sharing your posts. Set the **Sort by** dropdown menu to **Latest** before you save the bookmark, otherwise the results won't be in date order.

So, remember to include your branded hashtag in each LinkedIn post. And if you find that someone has shared your post, remember to say thanks!

Death by hashtag

Beware of the negative effect on readability when you use hashtags too often. Just because you've created some hashtags, don't cram them in everywhere. If you do need to use a lot of hashtags, it's best to put them at the end of each post, so that they don't get in the way of your core message. Hashtags in every sentence is the recipe for content with low readability. Don't do that.

Instagram seems to be the exception to the rule of avoiding hashtag stuffing. It's common to see 25 or more hashtags there. And that's one of the reasons why I avoid Instagram.

Branded hashtags versus generic ones

I recommend that you create at least one branded hashtag and use it to keep your business top of mind with your customers. You'll get better distribution of your social media content if you use generic but popular hashtags, such as #SocialMedia or #ContentMarketing or whatever's favoured in your industry. Check out Hashtagify[27] to discover popular hashtags.

You can mix and match popular hashtags with your own custom ones to get the best of both worlds: a combination of visibility with a personal branding element.

For example, LinkedIn's official advice is to post using

---

27 https://hashtagify.me/

no more than three hashtags. Perhaps you could use one popular hashtag and a couple of custom ones of your own. That's what I do and it seems to work well.

Your package names

It's easy to cop out and pick obvious package names for your services, such as gold, silver and bronze. There's nothing wrong with this and it's still better to have distinct packages than to present an undifferentiated service.

Remember that Content DNA means being the same shape everywhere. It means putting your true personality into every aspect of what you do. Why not extend that to the names of your packages?

Look back at your core values and think about names that you could riff on to create your set of packages.

As well as the names, think about how many packages to offer. Two or three is often the magic number. Offer a single package and you're not really giving people any choice. Offer lots and your audience may be paralysed by the options. But two or three packages is a good Goldilocks number to aim for.

Some businesses provide the illusion of choice by listing two or three packages but they make one of the packages a lot more appealing than the others, thereby steering people to take the action they want.

A tip many copywriters know is that if you want someone to buy a £100 package, you slide it up next to a £500+ package and watch people make the sensible decision to go with the "cheap" option. (And if anyone opts for the expensive package, you're quids in.)

I'd advise caution when using such psychological tactics. If you can deliver genuine value at those price points, it's fine. If you're playing people, that's not good

– unless "sneaky trickster" is one of the building blocks of your Content DNA. (If that is you, stealing this book off Ginny's desk when she was on her lunch break was not cool. Give it back and say sorry, you meanie.)

I'm mentioning the illusion of choice not so you can dupe others but rather so you can protect yourself from others doing it to you. While we're at it, beware also of the "double bind", where salespeople steer a conversation so that they can present you with a black and white choice between two options that don't really suit you. If you can pause for breath or even sleep on it, you should get the perspective to see what's going on. There's more about some of these psychological tricks in chapter 27.

Anyway, back to the package names: think of something aligned with your brand and that you could extend if needs be.

When I saw people talk about others (or themselves) being "rockstars" on LinkedIn, my natural thought for my LinkedIn profile review packages was "Backstage" and "VIP All Access". They're tongue-in-cheek but still clear enough to give an idea of progression.

Your email list

A common nugget of marketing advice is to build a mailing list. Why? Because email isn't subject to the same peril as social media. If your favourite social media platform changes its model, reduces your organic reach or otherwise becomes less appealing to you and your audience, you won't be as effective at getting your message out there.

But email is a different beast. It's pretty much the same as it's always been, and it seems unlikely to be much different in future. So long as people give their consent to hear from you, you have a direct route into their inbox. The only potential downside is that email providers may tighten their spam rules so that it's harder for your message to be seen. For example, Gmail users will know that mailing-list messages are often placed in the Promotions tab, which categorises those messages as potential sales spam. There are ways around this, though. It's a good idea to encourage replies from email subscribers, as that's a strong signal to the email providers that your message to them is of some value. Also, recipients can drag messages from their Promotions tab to their Inbox to re-categorise them, as well as adding your email address to their contacts list.

I recommend all of these methods when I send introductory emails to my Espresso email list. And that brings me back to names. Giving my mailing list a name has given it an identity.

When I created my mailing list, I wanted to get across that my messages would be short and sharp. As I write a lot about techie things, the idea of providing subscribers with a hit of "digital caffeine" felt right, and so I went with Espresso.

The branding of my mailing list means that I can refer to it with a single word and know that my subscribers know what it is. It's different enough that someone who doesn't know what it is might have their curiosity piqued when I mention it. None of this would happen if I used a generic term such as "list" or "newsletter". No one ever got excited over a newsletter. Remember, though, that the name is just a neat label. If what's inside the package sucks, you're wasting your time.

I hate the idea of selling and so I don't use Espresso as a way to push my services. Conventional wisdom is to send some form of sales message on every fifth email. It's OK to remind people of what you do but I never feel comfortable with making a bald ask like that.

And I know the naysayers will counter by saying, "If you provide great value in your services, you're helping people by selling it to them." I get that but it still doesn't feel right to me, and it certainly isn't fun. You know what they say: "If it isn't fun, it doesn't get done."

So, have fun with your naming and choose labels that reflect your Content DNA. The first time someone echoes one of your names back to you, you'll be delighted.

What you call yourself

I bet Lionel Messi wouldn't describe himself as an "expert footballer". Leave the labels such as "expert", "guru" and "visionary" for others to use about you if they see fit.

How you describe yourself is important. Focus on what value you can bring and be clear in how you express that. Let the praise come afterwards, and don't get busy trying to put a crown on your own head.

Now we're about to get into the thick of creating content. So, how long does it really take to do that?

26. HOW LONG DOES IT TAKE TO CREATE CONTENT?

People don't have short attention spans. Brands have short interesting spans.
– Mark Schaefer

Get to the point

The average blog post takes around four hours to write. Long content tends to outperform short content. People will stick around for engaging content.

• • •

Some people seem to rattle off content in minutes. Other people agonise over it for weeks. So, how long should it take?

It stands to reason that the more time you put into creating a piece of content, the better it will be. But that's thinking of it in terms of subjective quality, which, although important, isn't the be-all and end-all of what makes for effective content.

I've found an interesting difference in the success of my content depending on where it's published.

Content that I invest a lot of time in on my website performs well.

Content that I invest a lot of time in on social media performs poorly.

Dashing out a quick post for my blog (which I never really do anymore) doesn't get me any traction. And yet top-of-mind stuff I trot out of a lunchtime on LinkedIn tends to do very well.

Writing blogs

Orbit Media Studios run a yearly survey of more than a thousand bloggers.[28]

In 2019, respondents to the Orbit survey took an average of **3 hours 57 minutes** to write each blog post. In 2015, it was a mere 2 hours 35 minutes. So, the time taken to produce blog content has ballooned by more than 50% in just the last four years.

I'm one of the 19% of survey respondents who regularly takes more than six hours to create my blog content.

I am speeding up in some areas but it still takes a fair whack of time to produce anything that I'm happy to publish. For what it's worth, I don't see myself as a perfectionist, and I don't fuss over every possible typo before my content goes live. If it's something that can be fixed after the fact, I'm cool with it.

A print book is different, which is why I'll probably be re-reading all this stuff quite a bit, as well as trusting my editor, beta readers and proofreader to catch the things I've missed. Even then, something's bound to slip through the net. I wouldn't want to deprive people of their fun on Twitter, though, so I'll try not to lose too much sleep over this. That said, I'm not encouraging poor editorial standards in online content.

---

28   https://www.orbitmedia.com/blog/blogging-statistics/

More than 4 million blogs are published each day.[29] That's the bad news: there's lots of competition out there. The good news is that most of that content is pretty terrible. US sci-fi author and critic Theodore Sturgeon once declared that "ninety per cent of everything is crap". This statement carried enough weight that it's now referred to as Sturgeon's Law.

When it comes to web content, I think Sturgeon's proportions are quite generous. The vast majority of what's out there lacks depth and production value. So, what are the things we need to get right if we're going to stand a chance of producing anything of value?

Here's what I lob into my blogging cauldron:

Listening: do you know what your audience wants? Have you talked to them in person, by email or on social media?

Keyword research: have you done any searches to see what keywords are relevant to the topic you want to talk about?

Original thought: there's little in the way of original thought left but you need to do more than copy what others have already written. Can you put your own spin on what's happening in your industry?

Drafting: set down a first pass of your thoughts. If you've done the above and can avoid the temptation of editing as you go (one of the principal assassins of creativity), this bit can be quite quick. As direct-response copywriter Glenn Fisher says, don't write

---

29   https://www.worldometers.info/blogs/

anything until you know what you're going to write. In other words, do your research.

Multimedia: images, videos and infographics are some of the most time-consuming resources to create. And yet they can give your content a unique visual stamp and make it much more shareable than similar articles that contain text only. Would you be willing to put in the effort needed to create or source your own images?

Editorial: getting your thoughts down is one thing, but you also need to invest some time in formatting, editing and proofreading your content. Without this, your posts can lose credibility.

Before you ease yourself out of the room and go searching for an easier way to get your business noticed, do keep in mind the benefits of regularly producing blog content:

- **Less need to advertise**: content is a better long-term method of marketing.
- **Improved Google rankings**: people find you when they search online.
- **More satisfied customers**: your content addresses their questions.

Remember also that producing content for your website or blog doesn't mean that content can reside only there. Bits of your writing can often be repurposed and used as social media snippets, script ideas for videos, components for client presentations and talks at events.

Not squeezing every last drop from your content means

the hours you spent creating it weren't as valuable as they might have been.

How long should good blog post content be?

The same 2019 Orbit Media Studios survey mentioned above reported that the average blog post was **1236 words** long. In 2015, the average figure was just 887 words.

That means that average blog post lengths have increased by almost 40% in just four years. This makes sense, as the content is taking ~50% more time to write than it did in 2015.

There is an arms race of value going on. Content is the ammunition. Why is this extra effort needed? Why are our stockpiles of ammo getting bigger and taking longer to assemble?

It's hard to be sure but there's ever greater competition for content to rank well on search engines, and longer content tends to rank better than shorter content. And why is that? Because longer content gives writers more opportunities to include more relevant keywords that the audience is likely to be searching for. So, my conjecture is that more effort equates to better potential search rankings.

Longer content implies depth of thought, and it can make the audience appear smarter if they share something of real weight versus something lighter.

But aren't attention spans getting shorter, I hear you ask? Hard evidence for that is thin on the ground. The reality seems to be that we're becoming better tuned to spotting crap content. If the content is good, we'll go just as deep as we ever did. Guess what: people still read books. And now they binge-watch Netflix series. Some of us even spend hours watching livestream videos of other people playing computer games.

As usual, Mark Schaefer sums it up well: "People don't have short attention spans. Brands have short interesting spans." So, don't be afraid of creating long content. It can and does work, so long as it's engaging.

The most successful blog posts on my site tend to range in length from 2000 to 3000 words. I never write to a specific word count, either for myself or for clients, as that would encourage bad practice.

"We need another 807 consonants and 324 vowels in this column, Bob!" No, that's all wrong. We might want our content to be comprehensive, but it should still be as lean as possible. Filler is not our friend.

OK, so we've understood how long content needs to be and how long it takes to create. Let's now get into some details about making our content better.

27. HOW TO WRITE GOOD CONTENT

Me fail English? That's unpossible.
– Ralph Wiggum, *The Simpsons*

Get to the point

Your content is a conversation, not a lecture. Write the way you speak and stop trying to sound clever. If you'd never say it out loud, don't you dare write it.

●　●　●

This is the bit where everyone perks up in the hope of discovering the magic secret. I'm not going to promise that, but you should get something useful from the tips I give my copywriting clients on how they can improve their writing.

Headlines matter

As we saw when looking at social media headlines and bios, you need to convey interest, information and intrigue. This applies to content headlines in general, too. The job of any headline is to engage the audience enough for them to consume the rest of the content.

The headline is like an invoice. The job of the content

is to deliver the goods that have been promised by that invoice. Break this arrangement at your peril.

Unfortunately, grabbing the audience's attention isn't easy. Four out of five people who read a headline won't read the rest of the article.[30]

The temptation is to go for the sensationalist route. We've all seen it: clickbait rubbish such as "What Barry did next shocked everyone" and much worse besides. Headlines like this might still have a place in the trashy tabloids, but they no longer work on social media. Facebook and other platforms now reduce the visibility of such content, so it no longer pays to write like this.

Some article writers recommend spending more time crafting a headline than writing the content that goes with it. I wouldn't go quite that far, but your headline is much more than a label you slap on just before you publish. As you write more content, you'll get a feel for which headlines feel right and work well for your audience.

While you're finding your way, try checking your headlines via a couple of free tools:

- CoSchedule Headline Analyzer[31]
- Sharethrough[32]

These free automated tools give your headlines a score out of 100. They offer no guarantee that your headline will be good, but can provide a decent indicator that you're heading in the right direction. It's tough to score much higher than 60/100, so don't beat yourself up if you're not hitting top marks.

---

30 https://www.campaignlive.co.uk/article/eight-ten-people-read-headline/1374722

31 https://coschedule.com/headline-analyzer

32 https://headlines.sharethrough.com/

Some of my own headlines don't score brilliantly through such automated analysis, which either tells you that the tool has room for improvement or that my writing sometimes sucks (a little from column A, a little from column B).

Here are some sample scores:

CoSchedule Headline Analyzer sample headline scores (out of 100)

- 10: Business blogging guide
- 29: Twitter advanced search 2020
- 48: Business blogging: the definitive guide
- 53: The royal order of adjectives
- 56: Pen portraits: understanding your ideal audience
- 59: 3 false assumptions about Dropbox sharing
- 67: Martin didn't want me to show you this …
- 68: How to find freelance work on LinkedIn
- 74: How to improve LinkedIn engagement in 2020

Sharethrough sample headline scores (out of 100)

- 36: Business blogging guide
- 47: Twitter advanced search 2020
- 56: How to improve LinkedIn engagement in 2020
- 61: How to find freelance work on LinkedIn
- 62: Martin didn't want me to show you this …
- 64: 3 false assumptions about Dropbox sharing
- 65: Pen portraits: understanding your ideal audience
- 67: Business blogging: the definitive guide
- 67: The royal order of adjectives

Here's my best advice on getting your headlines right.

Add keywords to your headlines

The best headline reveals exactly what the reader is to get from giving part of their day over to scanning the remainder of the article. I think of the keywords people will search for when they're sitting in front of Google. This gives me phrases that are two or three words long, and I try to include those phrases in my headlines.

When I wrote about people's misunderstandings about sharing files and folders on Dropbox, my key phrase was "Dropbox sharing". When I wrote about advanced tips and tricks for searching Twitter, my key phrase was "Twitter advanced search".

There's no secret here: make the headline obvious enough that it sets the reader up for what follows.

Start your headlines with "How to"

This is a great opening when you're explaining a process. It makes clear that you're showing people a step-by-step way to solve whatever problem they have. Explainer content is my speciality and it works well for both written and video content.

Example: **How to speed up Google indexing**
CoSchedule Headline Analyzer score: 68/100
Sharethrough score: 63/100

Use numbers in your headlines, especially odd numbers

People seem to love numbers in headlines, especially odd ones. The best number seems to be seven. Dates also work well.

Example: **7 ways to increase web traffic in 2020**
CoSchedule Headline Analyzer score: 66/100
Sharethrough score: 55/100

Turn your headlines into questions

Try writing a headline as a question, the way a real reader would phrase it.

People tend to type short queries but speak much longer queries when interacting with Alexa and other voice-based systems. With smart speakers and voice search on the rise, we're likely to see these longer questions appear more often as article headlines.

Traditional example: **How long should my blog posts be?**
CoSchedule Headline Analyzer score: 66/100
Sharethrough score: 58/100

Voice-based example: **How much cabin luggage weight is allowed on an EasyJet flight in the UK?**
CoSchedule Headline Analyzer score: 59/100
Sharethrough score: 72/100

(Note: these headline-analysis tools might not be best geared to assess the quality of headlines optimised for voice-based search.)

Front-load your keywords

Put your keywords at the beginning of the headline and introduce the rest with a colon. This front-loading is considered good practice for SEO, and it seems particularly effective for headlines on YouTube videos.

Example: **Business blogging: the definitive guide**
CoSchedule Headline Analyzer score: 48/100
Sharethrough score: 67/100

Sensible headlines beat scandalous ones

Writing a clear headline can help your content rank well on search engines – and that's anything but boring.

If you want to exercise some creativity, move the inventive writing from your headline to your metadata description. That's the text that appears along with the title and link when your website content is shown in search results. You can also do the same for preview text that appears when you share content on social media.

Good metadata descriptions and preview text will help draw readers in – and it's better to put the clever stuff there rather than in the headline.

Let's look at other writing tips, now we've talked about headlines.

Be inspired but don't copy others

It's valuable to read up on what's happening in your industry but also to read more widely, so that you can get sparks of inspiration from different fields.

The worst thing to do is to focus only on what your competitors are doing and then create the same content as them. I'm afraid you just can't copy and paste your way to influence. If you copy good content, it's likely to have the fingerprints of the content creator all over it anyway – and you won't be about to get away with that.

These days, everything is a derivative of some earlier idea, so you don't need to panic about the need to be truly original. Keep in mind that even if an idea has been expressed before (and it has, because the internet is a big place), it won't have been expressed through *your* voice and through the sum total of *your* experiences. There will be people out there who want to listen to your take on things.

Give them the chance to hear what you have to say – but don't just rebadge someone else's thoughts.

Write without a filter

Start by writing down everything you can think of about what you want to say. This is how you create "the messy first draft". It's important not to stress about editing when you write your first draft. Focus on getting your thoughts out of your head and written down.

Even things that don't seem relevant are OK to include. You thought of them for a reason, even if you aren't conscious of that reason straight away. Perhaps they'll turn into something useful or otherwise help you with some other piece of writing in the future.

Writing in bullet points is fine during drafting. Don't worry about spelling, grammar or any of the usual stuff that you were taught at school. Ideas are the only things that matter at this stage.

You might find it best to write by following a template. For example, for blog posts you could use the following:

1. Headline
2. Question or problem statement
3. Intro and summary of key points
4. Key points in detail
5. Wrap-up and CTA

Whether you follow a structure like this or prefer to do things a bit more free-form, get those thoughts down and then leave the text alone. Take a little time away from the writing. Do something different: fix the shed, check the football transfer news, plan that European city break, whatever.

Then it's time to come back and edit without mercy, chopping out all the bits that aren't essential or relevant. It's like giving your dough time to prove and then punching the air out of it.

Leave only the content that's going to be interesting to the intended reader. Everything else must go.

Help the reader with good signposting

Executive summaries at the beginning of many Word documents are all that many people will bother with. Be respectful of your reader's time and front-load your text with the key points they need to know. If the reader doesn't get through the whole thing, at least they'll have got the gist.

A set of high-level bullet points at the start of the document is a great way to deliver the crucial info. Make the key facts clear and link to relevant sources of information.

Lists, subheadings and other visual devices are ways to break up walls of text, so use them to keep your readers engaged.

Write the way you speak

"Oh John, we can't possibly do that."

This is what clients often say when I suggest we put a dash of humanity into their robotic content. I guess it comes from the fear of not sounding professional.

Those same clients also say, "If only we could get our customers in a room, we could convince them to buy from us." Whether or not that's true, both positions can't be right.

If you ever do get a potential customer in a room and batter them with stuffy and boring words AND they still buy from you, then you've really lucked out. My bet is that most prospective buyers would be eyeing the door.

No real human would ask for a "transparent hydration

solution" when they just wanted a glass of water. So, keep your message simple and clear. And if you'd never say it out loud, don't you dare write it.

I have no high horse to ride here, by the way. It took me a few years of blogging before I started writing the way I speak. That's how long I needed to feel comfortable enough to let some personality show. You don't need to wait that long. You could start doing it right now. You probably won't, but you *could*.

If you want to give it a go, the best method is to record yourself talking about the topic you want to write about. If you have a smartphone, you should already have some means to record your voice. If not, search for any app that will allow you to record audio notes. Evernote is a popular choice should you need to look beyond your phone's built-in tools.

Allow yourself permission to talk without needing to be perfect. Don't bother with multiple takes or stopping and starting because of doing too many umms and ahhs. Play back your recording and listen for the natural turns of phrase. Much of it will be run-of-the-mill stuff, but you might also catch a few expressions you've never consciously thought about before. These are some of your markers and shouldn't be ignored. If they're not outright mistakes, be brave and make them part of your content.

For some people, the voice-notes method acts as their time-saving way of creating content. They record what they want to say about a topic, send the audio off to a transcription service, tidy up the text they get back and hit Publish. If you're in a busy leadership role, this may be the quickest and best way to get your thoughts out into the world.

Whichever way you do it, consider making your writing sound more like what real humans say to each other. If you want to build a congruent presence, you need to speak with a single voice.

Stop talking about yourself

Even if you write the way you speak, it's important not to make that writing all about you. Readers are interested in themselves, not in you. (All bets are off if you're an A-list celebrity.)

Steve Woodruff, the King of Clarity and author of *Clarity Wins*, puts it well: "People's radios are tuned to WII FM: What's In It For Me." Those people will tune out pretty quickly if your writing is full of "I" and "me" and "we" and "our". That sort of first-person writing is OK in short bios and profile descriptions. In your other content, it's a real buzzkill.

Arguably even worse is writing about yourself in third person – "he", "his", "him", "she", "her", "it". This is all rather detached and self-important, and it has no place in the production of relatable content.

There are legitimate uses of third-person writing, such as in legal and criminal contexts, but that's probably some way off from the type of content that's going to help you define and build your business.

So, drop the third person from your writing – unless you're very clearly embracing irony and charisma: "The Rock says you should shut your damn mouth." In software testing, we'd call this a limited use case.

The best approach is to make the writing centred around the reader, and that means using second person ("you") a lot. The writing wouldn't sound natural if this were all you did, so a mix of first and second person is most common. Look at the balance of what you produce and lean it in favour of talking about your intended reader.

Get to the point quickly

Start by telling your reader what they're going to learn. Then get on with delivering that message. Cut out the flabby bits and focus on the muscle – it's all part of the merciless editing process.

This doesn't mean that your content must be short. You might have a lot to say about a topic, in which case it's natural that some pieces of writing will be long. I've found that posts on my blog that are 2000–3000 words long tend to be shared the most (as well as ranking highly in search engine results).

Tell a story

You might be able to build a better emotional connection with your audience if your product or service can be wrapped in a business story. A common tactic here is to use "open loops" in your content. This is where you start a story but leave it incomplete until later, to help hold your audience's attention while they wait eagerly for the loop to be closed.

As usual, there's science behind this. Experiments done by Russian psychologist Bluma Zeigarnik in the 1920s showed that people remember uncompleted or interrupted tasks better than completed tasks. Now known as the Zeigarnik effect, this is a standard device used in films and TV dramas. Such shows often start with a spicy nugget that hooks viewers into sticking around to see how things will end.

Such storytelling can be effective in business content, too. According to cognitive psychologist Jerome Bruner, a fact wrapped in a story is 22 times more memorable than the plain fact alone.[33]

---

33 http://insightdemand.com/wp-content/uploads/2012/11/
Neuroscience-proves-stories-trump-facts.pdf

Honestly, I'm not mad about stories and storytelling in business content, but perhaps only because the execution is often so poor. If you want to use this approach, consider hiring a dedicated business storyteller such as my friend Katherine Ledger.[34]

Stop trying to sound clever

Don't be boastful or try to score intellectual points over your readers. Using long or fancy words isn't a good idea unless you're sure that your audience will understand what you mean. Writer and speaker Ann Handley said it best: "No one will ever complain that you've made things too simple to understand."

In a 2005 study published in the *Journal of Applied Cognitive Psychology*, Daniel Oppenheimer found that writers who used long words needlessly were seen as less intelligent than those who used simple vocabulary and plain text: "Anything that makes a text hard to read and understand, such as unnecessarily long words or complicated fonts, will lower readers' evaluations of the text and its author."

For the non-nerds who never look up references, take a moment to appreciate the majesty of this study's title: *Consequences of Erudite Vernacular Utilized Irrespective of Necessity: Problems with Using Long Words Needlessly.*[35]

This study shows that using fancy words doesn't make you look smart, and that doing so could make your readers think less of you.

---

34 https://copythatsells.co.uk/

35 Daniel M. Oppenheimer, Consequences of Erudite Vernacular Utilized Irrespective of Necessity: Problems with Using Long Words Needlessly, *Journal of Applied Cognitive Psychology*, 2005, DOI: 10.1002/acp.1178 – see https://www.sciencedaily.com/releases/2005/10/051031075447.htm

People remember and act on simple messages. This plays out clearly in politics. Look at these examples. In each, the winner's messaging was simple, clear and punchy:

- **Obama vs McCain**: "Yes we can" led Barack Obama to the White House in 2008.

- **Trump vs Clinton**: "America first" and "Make America great again" helped Donald Trump get elected in 2016.

- **Leave vs Remain**: "Take back control" meant the UK voted to leave the European Union in 2016.

- **Johnson vs Corbyn**: "Get Brexit done" convinced UK voters to back Boris Johnson's Conservative party in 2019.

So, keeping things simple can literally be the route to power. And simple messages can work in business, too.

But how do you keep your writing simple? A good way is to look at the "readability" of your text.

My favourite measure of readability is the Flesch Reading Ease (FRE). Scores range from 0 to 100, as shown below:

Score	How easy the text is to read
0–30	Very difficult. University/graduate level
30–50	Difficult. College level
50–60	Fairly difficult
60–70	Plain English
70–80	Fairly easy
80–90	Easy
90–100	Very easy

Aim for FRE scores of 60–70 in your business writing. This is considered equivalent to the reading ability of a 13-year-old. That sounds young, doesn't it? But remember the words of Ann Handley and Daniel Oppenheimer. Simple messages will help you win.

You can view the readability scores of your own writing by turning on the readability checks in Microsoft Word's settings. Once you activate this, you'll see readability statistics at the end of each spellcheck. Measuring your FRE score should help tune you to simplify your writing.

Another helpful way to look for complexity hotspots in your writing is to use Hemingway.[36] Paste in your text and look for the sentences marked hard or very hard to read. Making your sentences shorter and simpler will increase the readability of your writing. Trust me, your audience will appreciate it.

Use analogies

In technical copywriting, we have to explain by analogy. It's the quickest way to help people make sense of complex ideas. Using concepts that are already familiar to the reader, we bounce them off idea trampolines to take them pleasantly to new heights of understanding.

It feels a bit like cheating – as though you're stealing someone's homework and saying "See all this? This other thing I need you to know about is exactly the same, only with a few tweaks."

For example, I often tell people that "LinkedIn is like Facebook but for people who want to make money." It's a shorthand way of explaining that LinkedIn is in the same category of social media as platforms such as Facebook,

---

36 http://www.hemingwayapp.com/

but that it has more of a business angle. It's also a nice route into a conversation.

Similarly, I tell people that white papers are like blog posts but with body armour – they're bigger, stronger and better prepared.

You can use this approach, too. Remember this formula: "X is like Y but Z."

You might be surprised at how many people suddenly understand when they didn't before. Giving people that "oh, I get it now!" feeling is one of the best things about my work. I love helping people understand what they didn't before.

Give them just one thing to remember

This is another angle to the message about keeping it simple. If I throw you a tennis ball, you'll probably catch it. If I throw you ten tennis balls, you might not catch any.

Each piece of content you create should have one main takeaway. Even if you're creating a reference work full of facts and figures, there's still one key point you're providing: "Here's a guide where you can look up useful info about [whatever the topic is]."

Cramming too many competing messages will confuse your readers. As much as 75% of what you tell them will be gone from their memory within three days.[37] You'll have a better chance of them remembering just one thing.

Where you place your core message within your content also matters. Best practice is to put your most important takeaway at either the start or the end of your writing, because readers are lazy and often pay little attention to the middle. The traditional model is to build to a conclusion, hence leaving the important stuff for the end.

The modern web model is to give people as much value upfront as possible, hence putting the goodies at the start of the content. Of course you want people to stick around and read the rest of your article. They'll be more likely to want to do that if you don't drone on with an endless intro.

And even if they don't stick around, you've still served them well by giving them the information they were probably looking for. Somewhere in their subconscious, these readers are noting that your content helped them instead of wasting their time. Do that often enough and their conscious side might realise that you're the person to trust.

Listen to what your audience wants

Most businesses don't talk to their customers. They'll all say different but there really aren't that many meaningful customer conversations going on. You can buck that trend by talking with your customers and asking what sort of content they'd find helpful.

Sending out surveys and looking at data are all well and good. But what about direct one-to-one contact, either online or in person. When was the last time you earnestly asked a customer what content they wanted from you? Talk more with your customers and look for the simplest way to serve them what they would most benefit from.

Remember that this isn't necessarily what they say they want. As the famous Henry Ford saying goes, "If I'd asked people what they wanted, they'd have asked for a faster horse." This means that sometimes you have to take charge of seeing new solutions to problems rather than aiming to make incremental improvements here and there.

If you have a customer service department, ask them what real customers are saying about what they want.

I worked in customer service and quality assurance for a decade. Trust me when I say that they're an underrated source of customer insight.

Much of this chapter has been about simplicity, which I see as the absence of pain and friction. Find ways to remove all pain and friction from your business offering and your processes. Your customers will lap it up.

Use behavioural tricks

Copywriters know a lot of the sneaky back-alley shortcuts to getting the audience to take action. You can deploy some of this in your own content, too. Please stay on the right side of the line. I'm not here to empower con artists.

Reduce the number of product/service options you offer. "More choice" is a fallacy. If you run a market stall and offer strawberry, raspberry or apricot jam, that's enough for the brains of hungry passers-by to process. Bring out lots of other flavours and variations and those people will probably keep on walking. Just because a supermarket offers lots of choice, it doesn't mean your business should (unless you're in the mass commodity business).

Three options work best. There's something in our heads that appreciates the power of three. Try to offer three options where you can (like the jam), and note that the audience will probably be drawn to the "safe" option of the middle one. If the middle one happens to be the one you wanted them to pick all along, well, happy days.

Use price anchoring. If your product or service isn't cheap, you can soften up your audience by getting them to think first of something much more expensive than what you're offering. In his book *Influence*, Dr Robert Cialdini refers to this sort of comparison as "the contrast principle". People are willing to spend significantly more on a purchase than they would if they weren't exposed to such "anchoring" tactics.

I feel as though I'm stumbling into Defence Against The Dark Arts class now. As you can imagine, these and other psychological methods are open to abuse in the wrong hands.

If you want to learn more about this (and if you promise to be good with what you pick up), then read not only *Influence* but also *Pre-Suasion*, both by Dr Robert Cialdini. In the latter, Cialdini shows how people's thinking can be steered by what happens before you ask them to make a decision.

Most of us probably think of ourselves as being immune to such fancy tricks. But in experiment after experiment, the author reports that it is possible to get people to make the decisions you want them to. Below are some examples from *Pre-Suasion*. They'll get you thinking about how your messaging could be tailored to achieve the outcomes you want.

Remember: be ethical in your practices. If you're a salesy douche canoe, please skip to the next chapter and let's never speak of this again.

If you want someone to agree to try an untested product, ask whether they consider themselves adventurous.

If you want someone to select a highly popular item, show them a scary movie.

If you want someone to feel more achievement-oriented, show them an image of a runner winning a race.

If you want someone to be more helpful to you, show them photos of individuals standing close together.

Another interesting bit in *Pre-Suasion* mentions an experiment where subjects are shown banners on a website for buying a sofa. One banner showed cash to a group of subjects. This made them less willing to spend (because they were thinking about budget first). Another banner showed clouds to a different group of subjects. This made them more likely to spend (because they were thinking about comfort first).

There's a useful lesson if you're going to put prices on your website: don't use images of paper money, coins or credit cards! You'll succeed only in putting people into cheapskate mode. I fell into this trap years ago. I've long since removed such imagery from my copywriting pricing page, and it seems to have helped. Or at least, I can say that I get fewer pricing objections these days than I ever used to.

A quick digression now to make sure you're not caught out when listening to someone else's sales pitch. The following is a classic neurolinguistic programming (NLP) trick. Don't fall for it!

Because the words "by" and "buy" sound identical, verbal sales pitches often include sentences that start like this:

"By now, you already know that ..."

But the real subliminal message is:

"**BUY NOW**, you already know that ..."

If you're not tuned to these things, it's easy to be duped.

Let's end this bit on a high with a useful tip I learned 20 years ago when working in a call centre: positive language helps people make positive associations.

Compare "Sorry for being late," with "Thanks for your patience." It can take some practice to move from negative to positive framing like this, especially if your home life and schooling were geared towards being apologetic. But this practice is worthwhile and will help people think better of you. Keep in mind how your words make others feel, consciously and subconsciously.

OK, that's really enough of the behavioural tricks and tips.

Use power words as terminators

Sometimes, short taglines and statements have more impact when you move the most vivid, powerful word to the end. Here's an example:

When Marketing and Psychology collide, success happens.

A bit of word juggling turns the powerful word "collide" into the statement terminator:

Success happens when Marketing and Psychology collide.

Reordering statements like this means that the words are like a fuse burning away until they reach the bomb.

As with most copywriting tips, you can't use this for everything. In fact, in some instances, you'd want to do the exact opposite of this. Remember what I said about headlines for videos, for example, where it's often best to **start** with the keyword you want to focus on.

Finish strongly

One of the biggest mistakes I see when editing web pages and blogs is that the writer doesn't wrap up the piece with a strong CTA. Instead, the writing peters out – a missed opportunity. Content like this makes me wonder why it was ever produced.

The whole point of creating content for your business is to encourage the audience to take some action. For example, you might want them to read your ebook, watch a product video, request a demo or subscribe to your mailing list.

Whatever your desired end goal is, you can guarantee that your audience won't get there unless you give them a clear and frictionless way of doing so. Think about what you want the audience to do, and then create content that encourages them to do it.

Without a relevant CTA at the end of your content, you're wasting your time. Take a look at my blog posts to see how I handle CTAs in my content.

Though the main CTA traditionally comes at the end of the content, there's no harm in embellishing your work with CTAs at other points. But don't go overboard or you risk the content looking like a big sales piece.

Create a guide for your tone of voice and style decisions

You'll be best placed to be consistent and congruent in your content if you have a place to record all of the decisions you've made about how to write about your business. It doesn't make sense to try to keep all of this information in your head, so write it down.

Create a simple document and include words or phrases that you do or don't want to use in your content.

Even if you're running a one-person business, you should find this process useful. It takes some of the stress out of creating content, because you'll always have a list to check against before you publish new material. If and when you become a business employing several people, the style guide has an even greater role to play, helping to ensure that everyone who writes content for the business knows what's right and what isn't.

Because such guides are intended to be living documents, you can add and take away from them as you see fit, such as when new legislation comes along that changes things in your business or industry. A relatively recent example is the GDPR, which became enforceable in May 2018. Smart businesses were ready for this and had a handle on what they wanted to say about how they protect the privacy of their customers' data.

To be really grown-up about it, put one person in your business in charge of such style documents. Make them the "brand guardian" who knows your Content DNA and style decisions inside out, so that there's no delay or arguments if you're ever discussing the big picture or the fine detail of your content. Because Content DNA should apply to your whole business, the brand guardian might be empowered to speak on core business decisions. Note: they'll probably want a pay rise if you hand them this responsibility.

We've looked at lots of tips for creating content. Now, let's think about how to knock that content into better shape. That's where editing comes in.

28. HOW TO EDIT YOUR OWN WRITING

I'm all for the scissors. I believe more in the scissors than I do in the pencil.
– Truman Capote

Get to the point

Errors in your text will ruin your credibility, especially when they occur in strategically important places such as in headlines. You never know who might *not* become a customer because of poor perceptions about your standards.

●   ●   ●

Just as sloppy design puts us off, so does sloppy text. Effective writing comes from effective editing – it's like chiselling a statue out of marble. You risk losing credibility if you don't bother with the editing stage. As your business grows, errors in your text pose a greater risk to that credibility.

If you think loose editorial standards don't matter too much, check out the words of Matt Cutts, former head of the webspam team at Google:

"We noticed a while ago that, if you look at the PageRank of a page – so how reputable we think a particular page or site is – the ability to spell correlates relatively well with that. So, the reputable sites tend to spell better and the sites that are lower PageRank, or very low PageRank, tend not to spell as well."

That quote comes from a video Matt recorded in 2011.[38]

But even Google's latest support documentation backs up what Matt said all those years ago:

"Avoid:
● Writing sloppy text with many spelling and grammatical mistakes.
● Awkward or poorly written content."[39]

Google don't explicitly state that poor spelling and grammar will hurt your search rankings, but it wouldn't surprise me if these were signals they take into account when assessing the value of a page.

So, let's look at some ways to edit your own writing so that you can produce better content.

The golden rule of editing your own writing

It's important to give your writing some time to breathe, so always leave a gap between writing and editing. If your schedule allows for it, get a good night's sleep before you edit.

Don't be tempted to edit as you go. That slows down your writing and drains you of energy. Remember that one

---

38   https://www.youtube.com/watch?v=qoFf6Kn4K98
39   https://support.google.com/webmasters/answer/7451184

of my writing tips was to write without a filter: just get your ideas down.

Focus on your most strategically important content first

Some text errors are more forgivable than others. Will you be judged harshly for an error in a direct chat message? Almost certainly not. But what about if you made an error in your website headline or on the front cover of a marketing brochure or in an important product or service definition?

That's when eyebrows are raised and opinions are formed. "If they got that wrong, what else have they got wrong?" You don't want to be on the other end of that silent question.

So, please, right now, go and check that your key marketing materials – your website, social media profiles, brochures and whatever else – don't have any typos in highly visible places. You could be turning people away through such a simple thing.

I have seen people who work in public health write "pubic" health on social media, and I've also seen editorial professionals describe themselves as "poofreaders". It happens. Don't let it happen to you.

Don't rely solely on spellcheck

It's always smart to use spellcheck to help you spot "hard" errors – words where the spelling is incorrect in any context, such as *spayce rockitt*.

Even when words are spelled correctly, they're often used incorrectly. Compare these statements:

- We have an **envious** track record.
- We have an **enviable** track record.

Envious is wrong here. Using it like this means that your track record is – somehow – jealous. But *enviable* is right because it means others are jealous of your track record, as that's surely what you meant. (I say "you" but I don't really mean you, unless you've actually made this mistake, in which case you've stumbled on a free fix.)

Your spellchecker probably won't understand your intention, so it can't be expected to suggest a fix for a word that otherwise looks fine. The same type of inaction often happens with homophones – words that have the same sound but that mean different things (*way* and *weigh*, for example).

On top of that, words starting with a capital letter might be skipped by a spellchecker.

It's smart to use a spellchecker; it's not smart to *rely* on one.

Check for clarity and tone

A common trap when writing is to forget that you know the topic and you know what you really mean to say. But unless you set that down clearly, the reader won't get it. Remember, they're a reader, not a mind reader.

Clarity involves using the right level of language for the reader. If you know the reader is going to be comfortable with technical jargon, it's better to write in that style than it is to simplify into non-technical terms. Otherwise, you slip into pointless polishing.

As well as getting your message clear, you have to ensure your words set the right tone. That tone should be in line with your Content DNA – the building blocks that together form the "shape" of your brand.

Change your view

Hands up if you've ever written something on your computer, printed it out and *then* discovered an error. It's bloody annoying, isn't it?

We're more likely to spot errors in our writing if we can change the view of the words. This happens when our text is printed out and read. It looks and feels different from what we see on the screen.

Some professional editors and proofreaders still swear by printing out their documents to help them spot errors. I don't doubt that this works, but it isn't always practical and certainly isn't good for the environment. Also, measure for measure, inkjet printer ink is much more expensive than vintage champagne (watch series 3, episode 4, of Dave Gorman's *Modern Life is Goodish* if you don't believe me).

But we don't have to break the bank or the planet by printing out stacks of paper each time we want to check our writing. We can instead change the appearance of the text onscreen, and that gives us the fresh view we need to spot more wordy gremlins.

Here are some changes you can make to your digital documents when you're ready to check them for errors:

- **Style**: choose a different typeface that's easy on the eye.
- **Size**: increase the size of the typeface.
- **Spacing**: increase the space between the lines of text.
- **Colour**: change the background colour.

A good free typeface for making your text look different and fresh is Open Dyslexic.[40] It was designed to help people with dyslexia, and it's my typeface of choice when I'm hunting for text errors in Microsoft Word.

Pale yellow or pale green work well as background colours when you're changing your view of the text.

I suggest working on a copy of the document when you change the view, and applying fixes only to the main version.

Read your content backwards

Often, we read what we *think* the writer has written. We don't stop to check individual words or spellings. Our brain has learned the shape of common words and knows the structure to expect from most common sentences.

This is helpful: it means that competent readers can easily glide through content instead of analysing each group of squiggles in a Columbo-like crawl to enlightenment. As content creators, we can't rely on everyone being able to fill the gaps so effortlessly.

To make sure you've written the words you really meant, try reading your own content backwards. This will force you to slow down and check each word individually. It doesn't work for everyone, but it can be a good way to ensure that words aren't omitted or repeated by accident.

If you proofread on paper (or "tree meat" as I call it), you might also want to try turning the page around and reading the text upside down.

Read out loud

This must be my best tip for improving the standard of your writing. Speaking your words out loud helps you spot the

---

40   https://opendyslexic.org/

awkward bits that you'd say differently if you were really talking to someone about your product or service.

UK copywriting clever clogs Vikki Ross says, "All good copywriting is conversational." That means that if your writing sounds odd or stilted when you say it out loud, it's going to sound the same in the mind of your readers.

If you commit to reading every piece of text out loud before you publish it, you'll find that your writing style will naturally become more relaxed and conversational.

This will sound scary if you're used to creating more strait-laced content. That used to be me circa 2014, and my content back then wasn't much good. When I loosened up towards the end of 2016, that's when my content started to resonate with people.

If you want to save your vocal cords, set up your computer to speak selected sections of text. I've set up a keyboard shortcut for this on my Mac. Hearing my text spoken in the voice of "Serena" also makes it feel different, and that helps with error spotting.

Check your text when you're most alert

Editing your writing takes brainpower, so it's best to do it when you're most alert. Our bodies have different rhythms and you need to find the times that work for you.

I have a couple of "golden hours" in my day, from 11am to 12pm and from 5pm to 6pm. Those are the periods when I have the best chance of making my writing suck less.

Find your own golden hours and then reserve that time for brainy work such as editing and proofreading.

Break up the task

Read your content multiple times, each time looking for different types of issue. Here's an example:

- Reading 1: focus only on spelling.
- Reading 2: focus only on grammar.
- Reading 3: focus only on headings.

The more you break things down, the easier each reading becomes. This approach is great for improving the consistency of your writing.

Taking long breaks in between sittings can help you avoid "word blindness".

Phone a friend

Ask a colleague or a trusted friend to go through your document in as much detail as possible. It's best to request specific feedback. This makes it easier for you and your colleague.

- **Bad question**: "What do you think?"
- **Better question**: "Does the summary in section 2 make sense?"

Accept any comments with good grace and think about how you can make your writing clearer.

Don't chase perfection

Don't expect to spot every single error in your work. Don't get hung up about it either. If you can catch 80% of errors on each read-through, you'll realise that it's not worth checking the content more than three times. There are diminishing returns from editing that goes on for too long.

If you need to be sure of meeting a high editorial standard, the next tip is for you.

Call in the professionals

Most of your content might not need the skills of a professional editor or proofreader. But if you have mission-critical text that has to be the best it can be, you'll need the help of an editorial professional.

You could employ an in-house person but many businesses prefer to outsource such tasks to independent editorial professionals.

A vetted directory is often the best place to look for someone with the skills and experience you need. For example, look up the directory of the Chartered Institute of Editing and Proofreading (formerly known as the Society for Editors and Proofreaders – I used to be a director there).

So, you've written and edited your content. Next, let's look at repurposing and republishing it to make that content stretch further.

29. REPURPOSE AND REPUBLISH

Advertising is temporary but content is forever.
– Andy Crestodina

Get to the point

Get the best out of the creative effort needed to produce each piece of content. Repurpose and republish your source material in different formats and locations to make that content work harder for you.

●　●　●

Your website is your home base. It's the only corner of the publicly viewable internet that you can control. Social media and other platforms may come and go, but your website will always be there for as long as you choose to maintain it. That's why posting your business content there is always the best place to start.

But that's not where content publication ends – it's just the beginning. We've already seen that blog creation takes on average around four hours per post. If you're going to put in that sort of effort on a consistent basis, you want to maximise the value of the content you produce. And that means you need to do two things: repurpose and republish.

Repurposing is the process of turning some or all of a piece of content into one or more different formats. For example, you might start with a video. That source piece of content could be repurposed into a written blog post, an audio podcast and a series of quotes that are shared as images on Twitter and Instagram. From that single starting point, you've created content that spans a number of other formats.

This sort of content multiplication is smart because it can be turned into a standard business process and hence optimised. The creative work that went into the original doesn't need to be replicated when producing the derivatives. In a nutshell, repurposing means giving more legs to your source piece of content. The mechanics of how to repurpose your content would go way beyond the scope of this book. Should you need professional help, check out a service such as Content 10x.[41]

Republishing is similar to repurposing in that the creative work is done just once, but it's even easier and quicker because it doesn't involve a change in format. For example, you might start with a blog post on your website. That written content is perfectly good to reuse on other blogging platforms such as LinkedIn Pulse[42] and Medium[43]. We'll look at that in a moment.

Experienced content creators repurpose and republish their content because doing so lets them:

- Reach a bigger audience: good for finding new clients.

---

41   https://www.content10x.com/
42   https://www.linkedin.com/
43   https://medium.com/

- Create links back to their website: good for SEO.
- Reduce creative workload: good for saving time, because repurposing is ripe for being systemised.

Before you republish, get your content indexed

When you publish content on your website, it's not immediately indexed on the web. That means that a search for your new content will not be shown in the search results. Thankfully, Google is a lot faster at indexing content than it used to be: what used to take a few weeks now more often takes only a couple of days. But if you're as impatient as I am, you won't want to wait for Google to do its thing.

The good news is that the free Google Search Console[44] lets you submit each new page you create on your website for indexing. This means that your content might appear in Google search results in as little as a couple of hours. Now we're talking. You'll first need to register for Google Search Console and associate it with your website. The process is easier than setting up Google Analytics (another free service), but you might want to lean on a web-friendly helper if this sort of techie fiddling isn't for you. Once Google Search Console is set up, submitting a new website page or blog post for indexing involves nothing more than a copy and paste of the web address.

Republish on LinkedIn and Medium

Let's say you've created some content for your website's blog. Once your blog post has been published and you've had it indexed on Google via the Google Search Console, you're free to republish it on other platforms. This means

---

44   https://search.google.com/search-console

it's possible to republish content within a few hours of the original appearing on your website.

Now, here's where people get nervous. There's a long-standing fear of being punished for publishing duplicate content. Google and other search engines used to frown on content being repeated on the web. Such pages would be de-listed from search results and could lead to rankings penalties for the sites responsible. It's no surprise that this has filtered into the general consciousness of web users. But today, that fear is mostly unfounded. Search engines are getting smarter all the time and they're now good at determining original sources of information. They know that people are inclined to republish (or syndicate) their content in multiple places, and LinkedIn and Medium are common places for such republication to take place.

Of course, if you were republishing content in dozens or hundreds of places, that would send up red flags to the search engines. And if – heaven forbid – you were copying someone else's content, that too would be discovered eventually. On the assumption that you're not a spammer or a copyright thief, you needn't worry about duplicate content penalties from the search engines.

Speaking of copyright, don't worry that republishing your content on another platform means you're giving away your rights. If you wrote it, you have the right to be identified as the author of the content. The social platforms have various terms that allow them to reuse the content you publish in promotional ways, but that doesn't mean they own the content.

The act of republishing existing blog content on LinkedIn involves little more than visiting LinkedIn from a desktop computer, clicking "Write an article" and then copying and pasting the content from your website. The checklist below has some specifics to look out for.

You can do the same on Medium, using its "New story" feature to create a space for your blog post to be copied and pasted. Or, even easier, you can go into the Stories section of Medium and click "Import a story" to suck in your existing blog content.

Republishing checklist

Here's what needs to go into a republished article:

- **Header image**: reuse your original image. There's no need to reinvent the wheel. My images are 1200×630 pixels, because that size works well when the content is shared on Twitter, LinkedIn and Facebook.

- **Headline**: you could retain the original headline, but it's better to tweak it slightly. Doing so means you have the potential to rank in search engines for two or more different searches. It's like getting extra free tickets in the SEO lottery.

- **Body text**: use part or all of the original, omitting any complicated design bits, as these are unlikely to work on simple publishing platforms such as LinkedIn and Medium.

- **CTA**: keep this the same as the original. It's the single main action you'd like the reader to take once they've consumed the content.

- **Original link**: point back to the original article on your website, so that readers and search engines alike are in no doubt where the source information comes from. With luck, some readers will prefer to read future articles direct from your website – and perhaps you'll then have a new visitor and email subscriber because of that.

All this great content needs a means to spread through the internet, so let's now look at how to promote our content.

30. PROMOTE YOUR CONTENT

**The economic value of content that isn't seen
and shared is zero.**
– Mark Schaefer

Get to the point

If you make the effort to create content, you must promote it. Squeeze every last drop from each piece of content you put out into the world. Amplify or die.

● ● ●

There's no point putting a lot of effort into creating content and then little or no effort into promoting it. You have to do the legwork to get your stuff seen, else it will never fulfil its potential.

This is where having a good social media presence and a strong email list can really help. They give you a channel through which to tell your followers that you have something to share. If the content resonates with them, they start talking about it and sharing, and before you know it, lots more people get to learn about you and your business. That's the plan, anyway.

Optimise your content for shareability by including content that fits well inside a short social media post.

Consider Twitter, for example. Each tweet can be up to 280 characters long. Does your content include highly quotable content that fits well within such constraints? Not everything in your content should be a soundbite, else it might look a bit forced and lacking in substance. But the key ideas in the content should be easy to copy directly into a tweet for sharing.

You might also want to include social sharing buttons at the top and/or bottom of your content so that people can easily pass the message on once they've consumed the content. It's slightly worrying that a lot of people take little more than a glance at some pieces of content before they use such features to share it on social media. But if you're confident that you've produced something worth reading, you want to encourage as many shares as possible.

Sharing links to your own content

Once you've created content for your website or blog, you'll naturally want to spread the word on social media. I'm going to focus here on LinkedIn, as that's my social media weapon of choice, but what follows is broadly true of all social media.

One of the most eye-opening things I've learned about LinkedIn since I dived deep into it in 2017 is that social media posts containing links to external content get very few views. Why? Well, think of LinkedIn as though it were a big party. An external link is the equivalent of you coming along and whisking people away from that party so you can take them to your own party. LinkedIn's bouncers aren't going to be cool with that.

No, LinkedIn want you to stick around, keep looking at ads and eventually sign up to one of their paid packages. If you click a link and hop away from LinkedIn, well, you might not come back for a while – and that doesn't serve their needs.

This setup is bad news if you've got external content to share. Thankfully, there are a few ways around this.

Repurposing

The most involved approach is to repurpose your content so that instead of taking social media users away from their platform of choice, you give them a "native" experience where they are. This requires work, especially considering that social media is best suited to short-form content. If you've written a 2000-word blog post and need to squash it down into a tiny summary, that might take a while. And readers won't get the full gist of the content, anyway.

(Remember that you should be republishing long-form content from your blog as LinkedIn articles and Medium stories – but it's a stretch to go from long-form to short-form just so that you can avoid links in social media posts. We talked about repurposing and republishing in the last chapter – review if you need to.)

External link in comments

An easier method is to share links to your content not in the main body of your social media post but instead in the comments.

The issue with posting the link in the comments is that LinkedIn's default algorithmic sorting means that the comment containing the link might end up as the 7th, 42nd or 253rd item in the list.

It really depends on how popular the post is. Even for something that's moderately popular – say there are a dozen unique commenters – it's easy for the link-bearing comment to be lost in the undergrowth.

External link added as an edit

My preferred approach for sharing external links in LinkedIn posts is to use the write-post-edit method. This is where you compose and publish your post without including a link at all. Then, after the post has been published, you immediately edit the post, insert the link and then save.

This doesn't make much sense and when I first heard about it, I didn't see any way it could work. After all, the end result is still a social media post that points to an external resource. Why would that fare any better than a standard post containing a link? The answer is: I don't know – but it works. For the last couple of years, I've used this write-post-edit method to share links in my LinkedIn posts. My organic reach shot up after making this change. Perhaps LinkedIn will stomp on this workaround eventually (it makes me nervous to write it in a book, to be honest), but it's provided a great boost to my content over the past couple of years.

If you do use this method, be aware of a couple of downsides. First, your link won't be accompanied by a preview graphic, unlike with most social shares. If the visual is important, it needs to have been added manually to the original post. Second, links added as edits are displayed using LinkedIn short URL format (lnkd.in). If you're counting on people seeing the name of your web domain, this dilutes that branding opportunity.

When to post on social media

Whether or not you're sharing content from your website, there's no magic time for when to post on social media. The worst time to post bad content is any time. The best time to post good content is any time. The value of your message is far more important than the timing of your social media posts.

Remember that people will stay up into the early hours to watch things if they're good enough (that new must-watch TV episode, that hyped boxing match, whatever). If we can make our stuff that valuable, timings become irrelevant.

If you do still want to try optimising your post timings, bear in mind that this has a chance of working only if the following are true:

- You're sure that your audience is in the same time zone.
- You know when they're most likely to be online.
- You know your network of choice gets you good immediate visibility at that time.

If those conditions are true for you, perhaps you'll have marginal gains by putting out social media posts when you know your audience will be online.

Check your link previews

If you do share links directly on social media, it's good to check what they'll look like when your audience sees them. That's because when a link is shared directly in a social media post, it's usually expanded automatically to include the featured image associated with the link and a small snippet of summary text. If your website runs on WordPress, the popular and free Yoast SEO plugin will let you define which image and snippet of text will accompany any social media posts that link to a given page or blog post on your site.

You can check what these previews will look like in

practice before you publish any such social media post. Each social media platform has its own free inspector tool for this purpose. Use the following links and on each page insert the link to any page or blog post on your site to see what its preview will look like on that social platform:

- Twitter: https://cards-dev.twitter.com/validator
- LinkedIn: https://www.linkedin.com/post-inspector/
- Facebook: https://developers.facebook.com/tools/debug/sharing/

The bonus here is that these inspector tools ensure that only the latest image and text snippet is associated with the content. This means that if you've changed the featured image or text of a page or blog post on your site, putting it through the above inspectors will make sure that any old, cached version of the preview data will be flushed away by the social platform. I've strayed a little into the nerdy weeds here, but this process is quite important to know about should you ever rebrand the visuals of your website.

There's no magic formula

There are some things you can do to increase the chances of your content being seen on social media, but there's no guaranteed way of creating something that will do well.

No one knows everything about how social media algorithms work, so beware of "hacks" that show you how to get ahead. (Remember that my little LinkedIn link workaround above isn't guaranteed to work forever.)

It's highly likely that the social algorithms include an element of randomness in promoting the content that wins on their platforms.

Why? Shouldn't they just have a secret formula that would guarantee success if only people knew what it was? Well, maybe not.

Imagine you're a pigeon in a cage. In the cage is a button. When you peck the button, nothing happens. But if you peck the button again, you get a delicious kernel of corn. Peck it again – nothing.

Your tiny bird brain soon spots a pattern: you get a kernel of corn on every second peck of the button.

You can now chill your pigeony boots, safe in the knowledge that corn is available on demand. Your remaining brain power (if you have any) can now be devoted to other tasks, such as finding a way to MacGyver yourself out of this damn cage.

But what if you were in a cage with a different sort of button? One peck. Nothing. Two pecks. Nothing. Three pecks. Boom: loads of corn. Another peck. One kernel only. Another seven pecks. Nothing.

At this point, you're one stressed-out avian. You loved getting the early corn payload but you don't know when the next lot might be coming. You might have to do lots of pecks to stave off hunger before bedtime.

So, you do the sensible thing and smash that button. A lot. At the end of it all, you've lost count of all those pecks but at least you've got a haul of corn to show for it.

And that's all a bit like what content success can be like on social media.

It's not in the social platforms' interest to confer predictable success on you. They want you to peck the hell out of their buttons so that you keep yourself busy in their cage. You're paying them with your attention and your data, and they're showing you ads and other promos all the while.

So, keep this in mind if you're imagining coming up with a formula for content success on social media. It's always in the platforms' favour to introduce an element of randomness so that you are more likely to stick around and keep pecking their buttons.

The pigeon experiment is real, by the way, and our feathered friends really do peck more when there's randomness in the result. Look up the US psychologist BF Skinner and his "Skinner Box" if you'd like to know more.

The take-home message here is that there's no way to guarantee success in the casino of social media. The best strategy is to turn up regularly and be the same shape every time when you do: consistency and congruence.

Schedule less

Manual posting leads to better visibility and encourages more engagement. Stop using scheduling tools such as Buffer and Hootsuite to pump out content. It's much better to post less but to be present for the conversations that result from your posts.

I stopped scheduling all my social media posts in early 2017. This corresponded with a big increase in the visibility of my content. A big part of that increase was because I was no longer sharing links directly in my posts, as I've mentioned above. Again, social media networks hate anything that will take users away from their platform.

If you outsource your social media tasks to a social media manager, it's natural that they'll use some scheduling method to keep on top of the work, as they'll be serving multiple clients at the same time and it's not practical or smart to do everything manually.

If you have an opportunity to engage manually on social media on top of or instead of scheduling regular content to go out, you'll have a much better chance of making an impact and building loyalty from your followers.

Even if they knew you were truly present on social media during a regular slot such as in a one-hour Twitter chat or in a Facebook Live show, they'd know that they could reach you then. It's not ideal but any opportunity to build a direct bridge with your audience will help them remember and trust you more.

Much of my success on LinkedIn is due to my commitment to consistency but also to availability. I show up regularly and people know that I'm always around to engage with discussion after I make a post, so they feel heard and appreciated.

It takes some effort to execute this properly, and you might need to empower a junior member of staff or some other helper (one of my clients leans on his mum!) to do this. It's worth it, though.

A warning about automation

Be careful about the way you automate your processes. Imagine going to a fancy restaurant. You have the "back of house", which is where food is stored and prepped for service. You also have the "front of house", which is what's most visible to the customer. It's where the maître d' greets you, takes your coat, tells you about the specials and helps you settle in and enjoy the experience. The front of house has a little bit of automation (perhaps a printed menu and a card-payment machine). Meanwhile, the back of house might have a lot more automation going on. There are refrigerators, blast chillers, sous vide machines and meat thermometers – all there to support the chefs.

It's fine to automate many of the back-of-house processes in your own business, specifically those that don't detract from the experience offered by your front-of-house operation. (Automate the wrong back-of-house things and you'll end up serving microwaved lasagne and oven chips – see how far that gets you.)

But automating too much of your front-of-house processes will trample over the experience you're trying to give your customers. It has the potential to take your restaurant from being enjoyable, memorable and talkworthy to being boring, forgettable and purely transactional. Nobody raves about using a vending machine. Don't turn your business into the equivalent of that unless you fancy fighting the world on price (good luck with that).

Look at your analytics

Use Google Analytics (Behaviour | Site Content | All Pages) to see your best-performing website content over the last week, month or longer. Expand or riff on that popular content. It might be what helps you become known. Don't waste your time trying to improve content that doesn't perform well.

The mistake that I find some people make is to look at a set of stats from the point of view of "How can we make the poor stuff perform as well as the rest?" instead of "How can we make the best stuff really break through?" In my experience, it's doing the latter that strengthens brands and accelerates results.

Don't promote by tagging people to death

Tagging people helps to bring them into the discussion and gives them more exposure to your audience. These sound like good things. Often, they are.

But tagging should be done with caution. Here are some dos and don'ts:

- Tag someone in a post only when the content is highly relevant to them.

- Limit your tagging to a few people per post. No one wants to be a brick in your tag wall.

- Tag people in the comments as a good way to reduce their notifications burden (they receive fewer notifications than they would if they were tagged in the main post).

- Do not tag someone just to benefit from the halo effect of their engagement on your post.

- Do not DM countless people "just to mention you have a new post". That's one step up from mass-tagging them in public. Don't be a spammy douche canoe (a close relation of the salesy douche canoe we've already mentioned). Anyone from the canoe clan is getting burned hard in this book.

Talk to your email list

Your website content, blogs, expert articles and social media updates are all great for getting the word out about your authority in your industry. Along with all that, don't forget one of the oldest forms of internet communication: email.

Getting people to subscribe to an email list gives you permission to pop into their email inbox when you have something worthwhile to share. This is yet another touch point where you can convey your Content DNA.

Creating an email list is free with services such as MailChimp, and you might not need many subscribers to make it worth your while to produce the content needed.

Rather than reinventing the wheel and worrying about

producing even more content for a new channel, you take what you've already got and give people a taster of it by email. If needs be, look back at the last chapter for inspiration on repurposing.

I limit my Espresso emails to a maximum of 200 words, and the content is made up from repurposed information I'm already producing for LinkedIn and for my blog.

Putting the juiciest snippets into a plain-text email doesn't add much to my plate, and yet it's helpful to those who aren't online all the time, desperately scouring the web for the latest and greatest nuggets of copywriting and techie wisdom. Instead, subscribers know that, roughly once a week, I'll send them something helpful that they can consume when they have time. I don't dress up the message with slimy sales, and I invite people to keep in touch with me. I'm never more than a Reply button away from responding.

Industry standard open rates for emails are below 20%. So, if you create an email list and more than a fifth of your subscribers read your messages, you're doing better than average.

That doesn't sound too hot until you realise that perhaps only 1% or 2% of your social media followers will see your social content. In other words, your content visibility via email might be ten times better (or more) than it is on social media.

My email list is still pretty small but my open rates are almost always between 40% and 50%. A lot of my email subscribers also follow me on LinkedIn, and that's a good thing.

Rather than being put off by occasional duplicate messages, the people who see my stuff in more than one place are more likely to take action on the tips I share. A little bit of repetition can move people from "Hmm, sounds interesting" to "OK, I'd actually better do this now".

In his book *Content Chemistry*, Andy Crestodina suggests removing the word "spam" from your email signup form. I made this change to my signup form for my Espresso mailing list. Sure enough, my signup rate accelerated and I reached a thousand subscribers sooner than I was expecting.

In general, framing your messages with positive language is a good way to encourage your readers to make positive associations with your content. Compare the negativity of "sorry for being late," with its positive counterpart: "thanks for your patience."

The lesson is to use positive messages to reassure your audience and encourage action.

Gated content

I don't like the idea of putting content behind "gates" unless it's something you're genuinely looking to sell. And yet this is the orthodox approach for a lot of email lists: "Don't give them a downloadable PDF of anything useful until they give you their email address – and then you can spam them forever!" What a terrible proposition.

If the content is freely available *and* good enough to help people, they'll naturally want to stick around and find out more. It's no surprise that a lot of people now use a throwaway email address to do such web signups. It's enough to get them the content they were after, but they don't have to read whatever spam they might have been opted into afterwards.

So, before you get sucked in with ideas of using "lead magnets" to build the world's biggest mailing list, think first about what value you're offering. If it's really great stuff, do you need to hide it? Why not be confident enough in it to put it out there without demanding an email address from your audience?

If you show trust in them, maybe they'll show trust in you and go on to subscribe. This is my approach, and perhaps that's why my email open rates and engagement rates are way above what's typical for my industry.

The real secret to getting your stuff to move on social media

The killer app for visibility comes down to one thing: building relationships.

People often ask me how my stuff gets seen so much on LinkedIn. While I bang the drum for congruence and consistency, it's relationship-building that's the key to all my content and business success there. I do this in three ways:

- **Creating public content**: I create social media posts that spark conversation, and then I get involved in the comments. Ongoing public discussion spurs the social media algorithms to push my content out to more people.

- **Commenting on others' public content**: I look for interesting topics by others, and then get involved in their comments. Over time, those people reciprocate and hence boost the visibility of my own content.

- **Chatting in direct messages**: I connect with interesting people, and then get involved in direct message conversations. To take things a step further, I don't just chat but also look to introduce others that I know in my network to each other, as well as looking for opportunities to refer people for work. This turns me from being just another contact to being a hub. It generates respect, trust, even admiration. People who get those good feelings become avid supporters of my content and help increase my visibility further.

The last of these three areas is perhaps the most powerful. It's what gets people over the line, and probably takes the most effort.

What happens in the shadows of the direct messages goes a long way towards helping me succeed. It's the work that most people don't want to do. Though it takes me many hours each week to keep this up, I believe the long-term payoff is worth it: I build a network who I know, like and trust – and they feel the same about me.

Hey, we got to the end! Well, almost. I interviewed a load of smart people while I was putting this book together. The highlights are in the next chapter.

31. THE CONTENT DNA INTERVIEWS

The right content builds trust in your business, and businesses live and die on trust.
– Sonja Jefferson

Get to the point

There are too many goodies here to pick out just one. Spend some time soaking up the wisdom shared by these business owners, each of whom has carved a successful niche in their industry.

● ● ●

Before we wrap up, here are some insights from the interviews I carried out during the researching of this book.

Dr Ai Addyson-Zhang

https://www.linkedin.com/in/aiaddysonzhang/

You'd think a professor of communication studies might be stuffy, boring and obsessed with blackboards and sentence diagramming. No chance of that with Dr Ai Addyson-Zhang. Lively, enthusiastic and always willing to share what she learns, Ai is the modern educator I wish I'd had in school or university. With her #ClassroomWithoutWalls academy, she's changing the way education is delivered.

Like so many others, Ai used to suffer from Shiny Red Ball syndrome – the draining distraction of constantly being attracted by new things. Ai's breakthrough was to put her personality at the heart of her approach to education, and to focus on one thing rather than being a social butterfly. This meant she started creating more video, as it was the best way to communicate her personality and authenticity. I've long thought that video is the best way to bridge the gap between us and our audience, and this content format has worked well for Ai.

Ai's focus led her to the idea of a classroom without walls, and now to the topic of reinvention, which is her overriding theme. She's challenging what it means to be a college professor, a travelling and working parent, and a digital storyteller. Her YouTube channel is called Reinventing with Ai, and her current focus is on running ten-day immersion programmes aimed at cultivating a sense of entrepreneurship in her students.

One of the first things that interested me in Ai was her "3C framework". Those Cs stand for Connecting, Contributing and Creating.

"What I discovered is for anyone who wants to build a strong personal brand who actually wants to move their content around from one place to another place, they have to practise connecting, contributing, and creating. Whatever you decide to be, don't have a double personality." – Dr Ai Addyson-Zhang

Ai's 3C framework speaks to the truth about the way online communities work, as we looked at in chapter 19: Consume, contribute, create (I promise that I came up with my own model independently!). Her last line there about the double personality also chimes well with my mantra of being the same shape everywhere. People have to know what they're getting from you, and that's not going to happen if you always change what you say or how you act.

Branka Injac Misic

https://www.linkedin.com/in/brankainjacmisic/

Branka is an Australian marketing expert who works for financial services company GigSuper. She focuses on using fun and personalisation as ways of standing out from the boring status quo in the industry.

While other financial companies play a straight bat, Branka and her colleagues use video to welcome new customers. I've heard of this approach in other businesses, and video-messaging tools such as Bonjoro[45] are making such personal contact ever more accessible to everyone.

Branka believes that the human touch is what differentiates us from other businesses, and it provides a key advantage to smaller operations because bigger companies aren't set up to do the things that don't scale. This is the same important core message at the heart of Mark Schaefer's *Marketing Rebellion*.

You'll remember from chapter 27 (How to write good content) that one of the recommendations was to create a tone-of-voice guide and to assign a brand guardian within your business. In our interview, Branka was clear about the value of doing this. By gathering as much "voice of customer" data as she can, Branka ensures that GigSuper

---

45   https://www.bonjoro.com/

always speak the language of the customer. Often, this is quite fun and light in tone. As Branka says, "truth is funny when you can make it relatable." The language the team use reflects well on the target audience while understandably turning off some people. But as we saw before, marketing has to be like a magnet: it attracts but also repels.

Branka believes a tone-of-voice guide is needed as soon as your business moves past being a one-person operation. She also says that the brand guardian should have access to every part of a business, from customer service through to board level.

A clear warning from our interview was that brands that change quickly can lose trust with their audience. Sometimes, this can happen because they feel an urge to refresh so that they can stay competitive. In other cases, it can be due to a new face in the company wanting to stamp their authority by making sweeping changes.

Col Gray
https://www.linkedin.com/in/pixelscol/

Col is the brand and logo designer I mentioned when we looked at defining your brand values in chapter 9. He developed his own four brand values – empathy, honesty, creativity and education – after having been in business for almost a decade. If your business isn't that old, don't worry: there's still time to develop your Content DNA and set yourself up for success.

For Col, writing down his brand values gave him focus and led to a bigger vision for his business. He understood the sort of content he needed to create to serve his customers. It was difficult because it meant he had to say goodbye to some paying clients. It's natural to recoil in horror at the thought, but doing this can often lead to freeing up space to take on better clients. They're the people who buy into our sharpened vision of what we're here to do. They're apt to pay us more money, to stick around for longer and to shout about us to their friends and family. Hard though it may be to stomach, growth is rarely possible if we hold on to those we've always served. If we change, and we surely will, our clients may need to change, too.

Col said we needed to be consistent with the tone of voice of our content. It won't do to draft friendly guidelines for how to address our customers but then send them stern emails about account closures and other legal notices.

Because the costs of switching services are going down, we're in ever more peril of losing the customers we have. And yet the best source for repeat and renewed business is our existing customers. We need to show them love and to remember that the best businesses are fans of their fans.

Instead of developing products and services and then hunting for customers, we need to flip the script: searching for the customers we want to serve or are already serving and then thinking of how to develop something that serves them better or differently. This means talking with them to get to the root of what they'd really benefit from. A clear pen portrait (chapter 21) can help with this to some extent, but there's still nothing to replace real conversations. All businesses should have more conversations with their customers.

Col pointed out that giving the best deals only to your new customers makes your existing customers feel bad. It's fairer and probably better to give rewards to people who've been with you the longest. This might inspire new customers to come aboard, giving them the feeling of knowing they'll be treated well for sticking around in your "club".

Don't underestimate the goodwill that comes from your content having a positive effect on people. If you help people, they will be inclined to reciprocate (it's one of Cialdini's rules of influence). But even if they don't, they may well keep a positive association for you in their mind. When the time's right, the seeds you've sown could grow into the crops that sustain your business.

One way to stand out from the crowd is to consume content from totally different industries and even to go to events that aren't in your core area, to see what you can learn about presentation and how people voice their problems and challenges. If you want to learn about marketing, don't just listen to marketers. Listen to inventors, designers, artists, customer service reps, salespeople and more.

Eleanor Goold
https://www.linkedin.com/in/eleanorgoold/

Eleanor is a copywriter with a clear idea about her own Content DNA. It's apparent as soon as you watch the video on the About page of her website.[46]

Here's some of the text from that video: "Subtle and persuasive, not showy and abrasive. We do classy over sassy. Compelling without yelling. We prefer care words, not swear words. We story tell, not shout 'n' sell. We are anti-fragile, not resistant to change."

Now, you'd expect a copywriter to knock up a good

---

46   https://kreativcopywriting.com/whoweare/

script, as Eleanor has, but this also sets the tone for the brand identity she wants to portray. I've known her for long enough to say that what might sound like fancy claims are actually true. She knows her Content DNA and is showing up with that recognisable shape. "Subtle and persuasive" capture her well, and it's no surprise that this clear brand identity underpins her status as a well-respected copywriter.

Her tagline is "utterly compelling". She also uses "intelligent copy for smart people like you" and shares tips with the hashtag #WordsmithWednesday. These are all terms her audience resonates with and echoes back to her.

I asked Eleanor about the importance of getting these branding devices right. She said, "Define your brand early and remember that you have to kiss some frogs before finding your prince. Keep a note of what does and doesn't work."

"Changing your tone in different contexts shows a lack of confidence in what you're doing. So, once you start changing your tone, being serious here and bad-ass over here, it just doesn't work, and it looks like you're trying to please too many people."

"Don't carry on doing something that's not working."

That last point came up in a few of the interviews: the need to be ready to evolve our businesses. Real DNA changes slowly over time. For us to make Content DNA changes to our business, they're probably best handled in a gradual and considered way. The exception is when our business is small enough that we can be quick and nimble in pivoting. It's a luxury the big companies don't have. So, follow Eleanor's advice: define your brand early and change it if it's not working.

Dr Maitén Panella

https://www.linkedin.com/in/maitenpanella/

Maitén is a business psychologist and coach with a special interest in emotional intelligence. She helps C-suite executives, leaders and entrepreneurs to overcome emotional obstacles and unlock their potential. With more than two decades of business experience and a grasp of six languages, she's one of the most knowledgeable and interesting people I know.

We talked about establishing a bond between content creators and content consumers, and Maitén used her understanding of psychology and psychotherapy to explain how this works in her sphere. She told me about the concept of therapeutic alliance, which stems from Sigmund Freud's work on the theory of transference. This relates to when the unconscious part of a patient's mind decides that the patient should cooperate with their therapist. Here, the therapist is trying to establish a connection with a healthy part of the patient so that they can help them address whatever the not-so-healthy part is. This connection is based on trust, accountability and the idea of working together towards a goal. It can take three or four months to build that trust between the patient and the therapist.

Experienced content creators should be able to see the parallels here. We need first to understand the things that aren't working in the lives of our target audience. We then need to consider how best to make a long-term connection with that audience. This won't happen overnight, and our audience needs repeated exposure to our message before they'll trust us enough to listen and take action.

I asked Maitén how often we need to keep in touch with our audience. From the psychotherapist's point of view, she said that patients need to know that the therapist is there, but they must accept that they can't be there all the time. For coaching, she said clients would need a minimum of one session per month and a maximum of two per month. More exposure than this doesn't allow the other person to do the work they need in order to grow. Still, they need to know that they'll have support if they really do need it.

Again, we can relate this back to the world of content. We need to show up but that doesn't mean we should flood our audience with content. Too little exposure and people will forget us; too much and they'll be annoyed by us.

Maitén said that anyone can make a quick sale but that trust comes from building a relationship. This is another reminder that ads can be a useful tool in the short term but that it's content that leads to long-term authority and trust.

Mark Masters

https://www.linkedin.com/in/markiemasters/

Mark is a content marketer and the creator of the You Are The Media[47] community. I asked him what his brand identifiers were, and he answered in his typically interesting way: "I can't keep still."

In November 2017, a business mentor had told Mark that he sounded pretentious. He took that as a cue to start focusing on making topics easier to understand – and on being more relatable and likeable. This was around the same time that I discovered Mark's content. Whatever he did worked because he's definitely one of the most likeable people I know.

---

47   https://www.youarethemedia.co.uk/

Mark is best known for talking about creating an audience in a space you own and control. As content marketing became a saturated topic, he moved more into thinking about community and ownership. His "spaces you control" language has been echoed back to him – a good indicator that he's saying something that resonates with his audience.

His advice is to "become somebody that somebody else feels warm in front of. We need to be good, welcoming hosts so that people know the time they're going to spend with us is worthwhile."

There needs to be an effort to get this right because switching costs are low and it's easy for people to leave. By focusing on giving people the right feelings, Mark is building an emotional connection with his audience. Could they easily go off and find other marketing communities instead? Yes. Would they ever need to leave somewhere that feels safe and warm and friendly? No. Mark's approach is working, and he's creating something special through You Are The Media.

Mark ended our chat with a bit of pragmatism. Our time is precious and we can't do everything. Content creation such as drafting his epic weekly email newsletter involves personal sacrifice, so he advises us to be willing to give up something before we take on anything else. So, stop and think before you dive into another ongoing time sink: do you need to do it? And if you do, what can you drop to make it happen?

Nicole Osborne

https://www.linkedin.com/in/nicoleosborne1/

Nicole is a social media trainer and personal branding coach. Through her Lollipop Social business, she's built one of the best and most memorable personal brands I've seen. From the sugary titles of her packages to the bright colours of her graphics and even to the secret lollipop hiding in the background of her videos, she's really thought of it all. She jokingly refers to herself as "a German – but with a sense of humour", she's a smart cookie and well worth looking at as an example of someone doing things right.

It can be hard for business owners – especially the reserved Brits – to think that they might have a personal brand. But everyone in business has one whether they like it or not: personal brands aren't just for "Insta celebrities". The question is whether you want to take your personal brand (it already exists and you can't get rid of it!) and turn it into a congruent shape that's applied consistently.

When judging what to share and how to show up in her content, Nicole's golden rule is "would I want my mum to read this?" Her approach is to be "strategically authentic". Instead of being an open book, where all of your chapters are ready to be inspected, you can pick and choose the passages you want people to read. This idea of strategic authenticity didn't sit well with me when I first heard Mark Schaefer use the term. It sounded as though he was promoting some kind of contrived honesty.

But no, that's not what Mark was suggesting – and it's not what Nicole does. Being strategically authentic isn't about duping people or being fake. Rather, it's about being truthful in the things you share while not sharing everything about your life.

When you look at a house from the outside, you can't see through the walls. They're opaque. But you *can* see through the windows, and occasionally you might see people in there. They know enough to show only what they'd be comfortable with others seeing. That's why the car keys are rarely left in view and the bathroom windows are frosted. That's being strategically authentic. We don't need to see everything from the outside and neither should we be able to. People don't live in transparent houses, and that's just fine.

So, learn from Nicole: define a clear shape for your brand, but remember to maintain boundaries and be reassured that you don't need to share everything.

Stella Da Silva
https://www.linkedin.com/in/stellalicious/

Stella is an international education and training consultant and one of the queens of LinkedIn. As I write this, she's on a long-term project in the Middle East and is also contributing to one of Dr Ai's immersion programmes in Singapore. Both opportunities came about thanks to her LinkedIn network.

Stella's approach differs a little from the other people I've interviewed in that she doesn't have any significant "owned" space online. Most established businesses have a website or an email list or both. Stella doesn't. Instead, she's established herself through word of mouth and, latterly, LinkedIn. Her brand is built around being chatty, fun, caring and real. She has her own hashtags but is best associated with one that plays on her own name: #Stellalicious.

Her "being real" value is particularly clear in her content and when speaking directly with her: she's a strong, independent woman who knows her own mind and doesn't adapt her tone of voice for anyone. In her own words, she's "always 100% Stella".

As we've seen throughout the book, it's important to create a congruent identity and stay true to it. Stella sticks to her principles and that means people always know what they'll get with her. Some will like her; others won't. It doesn't surprise me at all that she has many fans on LinkedIn and that she's secured work opportunities there simply through getting to know people and having non-salesy conversations. It's interesting that she's been able to make this happen without a website, and though I wouldn't recommend that as part of a long-term content strategy, her example at least shows that this approach can work for some people.

In line with what I heard from Branka, Stella thinks it's OK for brands to change so long as they do it slowly. For the brands that many of us grew up on, such as Heinz, there would be an outcry if things were to change too much or too quickly. And to echo Eleanor's advice, if major changes are needed, it's best to make them early in the life of a business. A rowing boat is easy to turn; an oil tanker isn't.

Steve Woodruff

https://www.linkedin.com/in/swoodruff/

Steve is a consultant who helps train life sciences clients and smaller businesses in communications skills and branding. He has more than 30 years of experience in sales, marketing and leadership roles – and his special skill is in helping businesses find clarity. His book, *Clarity Wins*, is one of my favourite business titles.

Steve used a combination of introspection and bouncing ideas off others to help him identify what the building blocks of his brand identity were. He's now known as the "King of Clarity", a fun title given to him by marketing legend Chris Brogan. While Steve found it hard to embrace the label at first, because in his own words it sounded "boastful, arrogant and pompous", he now revels in it, saying, "It's been so unbelievably effective. The recognition has been huge."

With clients often addressing him as "King", Steve even has his own crown. (And it suits him, honestly.) This may sound silly but that simple "King of Clarity" branding device has been more impactful than anything else in getting Steve's clients to remember and take interest in his business. As I found with "relentlessly helpful", you need a hook that others will sing back to you.

Getting the clarity he needed for his own brand took Steve fully 20 years. He believes that we cannot be truly objective about ourselves, and he's often associated with the saying "You can't read the label of the jar you're in." Steve recommends that people get external help to "read their own label" and to speed up the process of getting their branding right.

Here are some of Steve's best tips:

- **Use shortcuts to help you steal memory real estate**: lean on people's existing knowledge to introduce a mental shortcut for the thing you want them to understand or remember. It's a common trick used to speed things up. For example, "It's like Netflix but ..."

- **Use vivid, short terms**: use tight, impactful words to deliver a message that sticks in the mind of the reader. Steve defines his own language, such as using "memory dart" as a replacement for "elevator pitch".

- **Create and practise your verbal shorthand**: make a "memory dart" that explains what you do and what value you bring. Practise delivering it in less than ten seconds.

Tom Albrighton
https://www.linkedin.com/in/abccopywriting/

Tom is a highly experienced copywriter and one of the co-founders of the Professional Copywriters' Network.[48] His book, *Copywriting Made Simple*, is a must-read for anyone looking to become a professional copywriter. In the book, Tom recommends that readers use three values to define the shape of the brand they're trying to build. With Content DNA, I'm suggesting you pick four or five values, to give you a little more scope for differentiation. But what matters isn't the number – it's the application of those values in a consistent and congruent manner.

Tom doesn't see himself as having a clear personal brand. I think that's just his British modesty coming out, but this speaks to an interesting point he made during our interview. For brands whose values include subtlety or modesty, it's natural *not* to make a big deal about *any* of their brand identity. While other businesses might publish their brand values on their website, a subtle or modest brand might not. Tom's personal brand feels of that ilk. He might not be one to talk himself up, but that doesn't stop me doing it on his behalf. He writes with humour and

---

great insight about advertising, both the commercial and political kind.

He advises not to choose boring "hygiene" values as our brand identifiers, as these aren't differentiated enough to produce a combination that stands out and is remembered.

Copywriters often think of and refer to branding and tone of voice as the written personality of a business. Although that basic personality should be the same everywhere (hence my drum-banging about the importance of congruence), Tom makes a useful observation about this: "We have to separate personality from occasion. We're different in the pub from how we are at a funeral."

Tom suggests that we think about how much flex there is in our brand voice so that we can talk in human language in lots of different scenarios. We don't want a brand voice that works only in highly technical contexts, for example, even if that is our product area. The voice has to come through every time we share a message. It's hard to apply consistency everywhere, especially in areas of compliance such as the GDPR, where a brand voice can have its life sucked out of it by an overzealous legal department. We might not be able to win every such battle, but it's important to retain our shape as much as we can.

Tom thinks it's good for brands to evolve so long as doing so reflects the way people perceive them and talk about them. For example, some older Brits may recall the subtle and sensible transition of one of the nation's favourite supermarkets from J Sainsbury to Sainsbury's.

But such shifts often don't work when nobody has asked for or needs them. Examples include the rebrands by Weight Watchers (mentioned in chapter 15), Dropbox and

Royal Mail. The last of these included a £1.5 million rebrand to Consignia in 2001, followed a year later by a £1 million re-rebrand back to Royal Mail.

Tracey Tait

https://www.linkedin.com/in/traceytait/

Tracey is an independent marketing consultant who focuses on the value of conversations as the route to new business. A former marketing manager for Nike, Tracey's dumped her old robotic corporate self and replaced it with a more relaxed, approachable presence that's in keeping with her true self. She now has a chatty and fun personal brand that helps businesses get conversions without pushy sales. She serves those who've followed her in ditching the corporate world and starting their own business. And she's never far from a cup of tea – it's a deliberate part of her brand.

As other interviewees have said, Tracey has noticed that clients have started to echo her brand identity and language. She added "Conversations to Conversions" to her marketing message in the middle of 2019 and started seeing new clients mentioning it back to her. This took her aback at first but now it's a clear signal that she's connecting with people the right way and making a difference to them.

Tracey also sees other positive signals, such as when clients label her a mind reader or ask how she knew exactly what they were struggling with. This all reveals someone who's in tune with the needs of her customers. The best way to do the same in your own business is to keep looking for clues in the emails you exchange with customers and, of course, to talk with them as regularly as you can and to listen with intent. The more they see you as a genuine helper and partner, the less they'll resist buying your product or service.

Tracey's advice is to keep your language simple and avoid jargon unless you're sure that your audience will understand it. This comes back to knowing the audience well enough to appreciate what will work for them. If they expect and want heavy, technical terms, that's what to give them. But judge the audience's need incorrectly and you risk closing off all opportunities for meaningful conversation.

With so many of our first introductions happening online, Tracey says that every piece of content we create should be thought about as potentially the first time someone "meets" us. We need to show the real us at all times rather than a cardboard cut-out version. Tracey also believes that being the same shape everywhere increases the sense of trust and intimacy we have with our audience. They get to know, like and trust us. That trust leads to them spending more time consuming our content and eventually becoming loyal customers.

32. LET'S WRAP UP

There is no greatness where there is no simplicity, goodness and truth.
– Leo Tolstoy

Get to the point

Make consistency and congruence the foundation for everything you do. Start now.

● ● ●

In school, we learn to build our writing towards the big conclusion. I've written for the web for so long that it's now ingrained in me to deliver the value upfront, with the impatient reader in mind. So, let's keep it short and sweet.

Think about the handful of building blocks that make up your true Content DNA. What are the authentic and differentiated values that give your brand its shape? What does your stencil really look like?

When you have that clear in your mind, you'll find it so much easier to identify your anchor value – the one thing you want people to have in mind when they think of you – and the tagline that defines your business.

Getting this right means your content will always have a style that's recognisably you. It'll be the stuff that your poison portrait will hate but that your pen portrait will lap up.

And if you stick at it for long enough, you'll encourage more and more lurkers to step out from behind the velvet rope. Most of all, you'll be known, remembered and trusted as being the go-to source of information in your industry.

Now, imagine that's really you in a few years. If you want to make it happen, you have the tools. Make consistency and congruence the foundation for everything you do, then use your Content DNA building blocks to shape your territory.

It's time to get to work.

ABOUT THE AUTHOR

This bit's always written in third person, but I can't bring myself to do that and I'm not important enough to have someone else write it for me. I'm a technical copywriter, which is a fancy title for someone who writes the words that go on business websites. I write explainer content for clients who are too busy or too close to their business to do it themselves.

I'm an Apple fanboi based in South Wales, UK, and chose techie tinkering as a way of life when it became apparent that I had neither the aptitude nor dietary discipline to play for Liverpool FC. If you ever want to chat about writing or football, I'm easy to look up online.

INDEX